THE GIANT KILLERS

By the same author

HARDAKER OF THE LEAGUE
SOCCER CHOICE (with Ron Greenwood)

THE GIANT KILLERS

Bryon Butler

'And there went out a champion out of the camp of the Philistines named Goliath of Gath whose height was six cubits and a span . . . David prevailed with a sling and with a stone.'

1 *Samuel*, 17.

PELHAM BOOKS
LONDON

To Mum and Dad

First published in Great Britain by
PELHAM BOOKS LTD
44 Bedford Square
London WC1B 3DU
1982

British Library Cataloguing in Publication Data
Butler, Bryon
The giant killers
1. F.A. Cup—History
I. Title
796.334'64 GV944.G7

ISBN 0 7207 1371 4

Printed and bound in Great Britain by
Billing & Sons Ltd, Guildford, London, and Worcester

Contents

Acknowledgements

For help along the way, my sincere thanks to, among many others, Howard Peters, Paul Plowman, Colin Cameron, Bill Miles, David Foot, Brian W. Moore, John Parsons and Martin Dean.

Foreword by Denis Law

I think it is high time the Giant Killers had a book all to themselves. Millions of words are written about FA Cup finalists, but to my knowledge this is the first to be dedicated to the little clubs who provide everyone with so much fun each year.

It can be argued that some of the small clubs who have beaten their betters have made more of a mark on the history of the game than many who have reached Wembley. Most people with an interest in football know that Walsall beat mighty Arsenal in 1933, but how many can tell you who won the Cup that year?

I speak with personal experience of the pain these little chaps can cause. I was a member of the Manchester United side which won the League championship by four points in 1967 – and yet that same season we were beaten 2-1 by Norwich in the fourth round of the Cup at Old Trafford. Norwich were struggling in the lower half of the Second Division but they were the only side that season to win on our ground. In the previous five seasons we had won the Cup once and reached the semi-finals four times, and the following season we won the European Cup. But on that day in 1967 we lost at home to a side all the pundits said we were going to eat alive. Impossible . . . but it happened! I was so ashamed and disgusted, I stayed indoors for about a week.

We took things too casually, we assumed we would win and we paid the price in full. Our attitude was wrong, and so the fact that we had better players did not count for much. That, I think, is the reason for many upsets.

Oddly enough, Norwich were the first giant killers I noticed. That was in 1959 when I was eighteen and playing for Huddersfield. Bill Shankly was our manager and I went with him to watch Sheffield United, who were then a very good Second Division side, play Norwich – in their Division Three days – at Bramall Lane. The result was a 1-1 draw, but Norwich won the return and rounded off a magnificent Cup run by taking Luton to a replay in the semi-finals.

The Cup didn't mean too much to me then. I was young and had only been playing in English football for a couple of seasons. The magic of the tournament hadn't got through to me – but it did in 1963 when we won the Cup by beating Leicester in the final. In fact, our win was an upset in its own right. Leicester were a very good side then, and even had a chance of completing the 'double'. They finished fourth from the top of Division One and we ended fourth from the bottom. But we beat them in the final and afterwards I said: 'I won't mind if I never play at Wembley again. I've been here and won.' It was my very first medal in professional football and I can still taste the joy of that victory. There is nothing to compare with a winning day at Wembley.

I sometimes hear it said that the little clubs should not be allowed to compete in the Cup and that it should be confined to League clubs, just as the League Cup is. What nonsense! The FA Cup is the property of everyone in football, big and small, professional and amateur, and that is the secret of its success. Everyone has a share in its ups and downs, and that is why we all love it.

Introduction

One of the FA Cup's most compelling quarter-hours takes place in a large, cheerful room at Lancaster Gate, the home of the Football Association, during the second or third week of every December. Outside, about half the length of a pitch away, there is the drumming infinity of traffic on the Bayswater Road; inside there is not a footballer in sight.

It is the draw for the Third Round proper of the Cup, the round in which the 44 clubs of the Football League's First and Second Divisions are joined by 20 others of lesser means and humbler pedigree. The 20 have sharp-elbowed their way to the front of nearly 400 others who compete for the Cup each season the 48 clubs of the Third and Fourth Divisions, who enter the lists at the time of the First Round proper, plus a ragtime army of optimists from every nook and cranny of the country. There may even be a club there which has clawed its way through from the earliest qualifying rounds in September.

The democracy of the Cup is now at work. The venerables of the Cup committee, guarantors of the honesty of it all, watch as sixty-four numbered boxwood balls are placed in a blue velvet bag, given a hearty shake and solemnly drawn out – two at a time. The ocean Titans of the game are taking their chance with its pond-dwellers.

Good fortune now can mean a fortune of a more tangible kind later on. It is important to the clubs whose turnover runs into millions, but perhaps even more so to those who can hardly afford to give visitors a half-time cup of tea. To the big it can mean prosperity, to the small it may promise survival. But there is much more than money involved. The Cup is important for its own sake. There is a sense of adventure and fantasy in the air.

The excitement is built in to a procedure which has never changed. Herbert Chapman of Arsenal, arguably the greatest of all managers, wrote fifty years ago: 'To succeed in the Cup you want luck, a deal of it, not so much perhaps on the field as in the

Council chamber where ties are fortuitously arranged. There are times, especially when it goes against you, when you are inclined to believe that too much luck enters into the tournament. Personally, however, I would not have the conditions altered. Indeed, to tinker with them would rob the event of much of its fascination.'

The secret of the Cup lies in those 'conditions'. They are the whole charm of the tournament and the essence of its popularity. It is the importance of luck which, as the Cup committee waits for the draw to start, fills the room with a heavy silence.

Peer will be drawn against peer, but Arsenal versus Manchester United versus Liverpool versus Nottingham Forest versus Ipswich versus Aston Villa versus any other First Division club, will raise no more than a murmur of interest at this stage of the tournament. Home advantage is important but games between clubs of this stature are standard roses which can be enjoyed at any time of the season.

It is something else they are all waiting for, something that will sound like this: 'Number 27 . . . Colchester United' – will play – 'Number 9 . . . Leeds United.' Or, perhaps, Altrincham will be drawn at home to Liverpool, or Yeovil to Arsenal, or Crewe to Tottenham. Then there will be nudges and winks and a buzz in the chamber, a reaction that will immediately be echoed by cheers at the ground of the small, lucky club as the draw is relayed to them by radio. Excited but unknown players clustered around a transistor are one of the traditional pictures of the Cup.

Those players know, as the country knows, that soon they will be celebrities. The Cup has pushed them into the centre of the stage and it will soon be common knowledge that, in between football matches, they deliver milk, design bungalows, drive buses, collect tax or even draw dole. There will be public appearances and private opportunities for making money. There will be reporters and photographers, radio and television, business offers, autograph hunters, hangers-on and jangling telephones. There will be 'special' training and 'secret' plans.

There will also be hope, which may even become conviction,

that on the day itself they will confound football and upset the natural order of things. They will be told 'the Cup is a great leveller', 'Cup football is different', 'fortune favours the brave', and that match-day is 'the greatest day in our history'.

They will be told to remember great deeds of the past: names that sound like battle honours will be rolled out . . . Swindon, Walsall, Yeovil, Norwich, Oxford, Bournemouth, Peterborough, Colchester and, later on, Harlow, Blyth Spartans, Bath, Leatherhead, Hereford, Wimbledon, Wycombe Wanderers, Enfield and Exeter. They will be told that the impossible is always possible in the Cup, that six non-League clubs took part in the third round in 1978 and that five Third Division clubs have reached the semi-finals.

Somewhere, inevitably, they will read that the age of the giant killer is over, a piece of bread-pudding logic that will have something to do with high wages, increased professionalism and a growing gap between the big and small. Players have been reading similar stuff for fifty years but nobody has taken it to heart. They will even read that the game's little people have no right to be in the Cup at all and that it should be strictly the preserve of the League clubs. A First Division manager with little sense of history, no heart and a cute turn of phrase may be reported as saying: 'Blyth Spartans? What are they . . . tin soldiers you get with the cornflakes?' or 'Barnet? That reminds me of hairnets, not football.' Our potential heroes are recommended to laugh with the rest. Giant killing is often a case of answering insult with injury.

Every year, too, it is explained exactly why small clubs sometimes overcome their elders and betters. Alec Stock, who played and managed Yeovil to victory over Sunderland soon after the Second World War, says simply: 'If big clubs accepted the fact that they can be beaten by little clubs there would not be many giant killers, but too many do not want to run and sweat. They do not always appreciate that skill is only decisive if two teams are working equally hard. If all 22 players in a game give everything then skill, like cream, will rise to the top.'

Complacency is one factor, then, but Danny Blanchflower, who observed life from the heights of Tottenham, suggests another reason:

I am convinced fear tips the scales in favour of the underdog. Nobody wants to get behind the pack. Nobody wants to lose. So the order of the day is: 'Be careful boy. Don't take any chances.' The big fellow is fighting against himself as well as those upstarts who are racing and dashing about all over the place with nothing to lose and nobody to belittle them if they do. The little guy with no fears and responsibility goes mad and turns the game into a riot where anything can happen and usually does. He finds hidden strength to inspire his carefree frolics and he generates a tremendous unnatural pace into the game.

Blanchflower was in the Spurs team beaten by Norwich, then of the Third Division, in 1959.

Luck comes into it: the kind of luck which is deserved – 'We make our own luck, lad' – and the kind of luck which has more to do with lucky boots, lucky socks, lucky ties, lucky golliwogs, lucky things to say, lucky people to touch, lucky meals, lucky hotels and lucky positions in which to run out onto the field . . . all geared to marshal the forces of the supernatural or, at least, provide a slice of providential insurance to be drawn on when the going gets tough.

Luck can be half the width of a goal-post, a moment's insanity by an opponent, or even a pair of torn trousers. Don Revie's Leeds United once lost a Cup-tie after the trousers of a 'lucky' blue suit had protested in the only way they knew how against a sudden, stretching movement. They split. Revie was obliged to change – and his team went down with a bump. Together they stood, divided they fell. Luck may shape a Cup draw, but is it luck when the celebrated forwards of a major club hit the crossbar of their little rivals half a dozen times and still fail to score? That is more about bad shooting than bad luck. Successful managers refuse to acknowledge the word, unsuccessful managers depend on it.

Tradition is a more tangible thing. The present can draw on the past as surely as a barman draws off a pint from the wood. It is something which creeps into the bricks and mortar of a club, something which sustains and inspires when the moment is right. Yeovil Town are a good example, a non-League club which has had good and bad sides down through the years, but when it comes to the Cup, then, as Alec Stock says, the players, pitch, goal-posts, corner-flags and stands unite. They have reached the Third Round on nine occasions, more than any other non-League club, and who would choose to argue that their early successes had nothing to do with their celebrated moments twenty and thirty years on. Some clubs, living for the hour, have a single glimpse of glory; but Yeovil's triumphs bridge generations. Clubs like this come alive when they turn to the Cup. They hear bugles and smell gunpowder. The hills and streets are alive with the clamour of battle. 'There is no humility in the Cup,' said Herbert Chapman.

The big clubs know that challenges of this kind are to be avoided at all costs. They know it may involve a journey to a ground and probably a town they don't know, to a corner of dockland, or to well-heeled commuter country, or to windy space on the edge of a moor or through back-to-back terraces in down-town anywhere. They may then have to change in a dressing-room like a gardener's shed, run out in front of spectators smacking their lips like flesh-eaters and square up to muscle-bound opponents who are prepared to die for their cause.

That, at least, is always the romantic view; the reality can be different. Many small clubs these days have neat, well-equipped grounds, their methods are intelligently considered and their teams generously stocked with players of ability and pedigree, often past their best but able for ninety minutes on the right day to find new heart and legs. The gap between big and small will be further narrowed if the referee believes there is one set of laws for Cup football and another for League, if he grants the underdogs a licence to bruise and up-end in a way he wouldn't dream of allowing on an ordinary Saturday. 'Typical Cup football' is not always as heroic as it sounds. The dice can be loaded in favour of the little chap.

But, such nagging considerations aside, the romance of the giant killers endures. Their deeds enrich and illuminate our winters. Big clubs are expected to win things and they form an orderly queue as they wait their turn, but once or twice in most seasons an underdog crosses the game's precisely defined social boundaries. A mouse roars and the nation listens.

Giant killers are also to be observed in the World Cup, the various European tournaments, the League Cup and every other competition devised by man, but shocks in the FA Cup somehow shock most of all. In the beginning was the Cup and, in stature and manner, it is still the daddy of them all.

This is an affectionate tribute rather than a detailed history. I have started our story with Darwen, a team of Lancashire mill-workers who ruffled the gentry more than a hundred years ago when the game was young, and I have then selected one example of giant killing from each of the decades of this century. Selection was interestingly difficult, and I hope the ingredients and essential truths of the examples chosen will stir the memories of all those who were not.

Bryon Butler
Guildford, 1982

1 Darwen...1879

The Cup was still an infant when it discovered the first of its iconoclasts in the Lancashire valley-town of Darwen. The local football team did not topple their giant; but they made the big fellow totter. They established the democracy of the tournament.

The young mill-workers of Darwen genuinely astonished the sprouting world of football in the early months of 1879 by reaching the fourth round of the Cup, the quarter-final stage, where they stretched one of the game's original giants, the Old Etonians, to their limits. It took three games full of drama and tension at Kennington Oval to settle the issue. The first was drawn 5-5, with Darwen scoring four in the last quarter-hour, the second was again drawn, 2-2 after extra time, and it was only then, drained and dispirited by the travelling, that the Darruners were overcome. A tradition was born.

The context of Darwen's success is important. Football had been picked up off the gas-lit streets of the country by the universities, schools and officers' messes of the south. The game at its highest and most organized levels belonged to the privileged, to the Wanderers and the Royal Engineers, Oxford University and the Old Etonians. Others were to take their turn: Lancashire was the dominant force from 1883 to 1893, the Midland counties asserted themselves as the old century gave way to the new and later came the turn of the southern professional clubs. But even in 1879, the year of Darwen, it was evident that the masses were about to take the game from the upper classes. Virgil and the birch were making way for a tide of cloth caps.

Charles Alcock, the first paid secretary of the fledgeling Football Association, captain of the Wanderers when they became the first winners of the Cup in 1872 and one of the game's father-figures, recognized that 'what has been the recreation of a few is now becoming the pursuit of thousands, an athletic exercise carried on under a strict system and in many cases by an enforced term of training, almost magnified into a profession.' Then thousands . . . now, a girdle round the earth, tens of millions.

Darwen, however, had no vision of all this. The town is coddled and isolated in one of those finger-like ridges thrown up on the side of the Pennines, a community which has spread naturally up the softer and broader slopes to its west. The roads out reach for the sky, many leading to the dark and gnarled beauty of Darwen Moor, and its people have often woken to find themselves entombed by winter.

Today Darwen is a place of gentle charm, small, independent, its character re-defined rather than raped by the modern architect and developer. Commuters from Manchester, twenty miles to the south-east, have discovered the town, but its past and present are still nicely in step. There is Victoriana, but also paint, perspex, cotton and wall-paper.

Darwen's population in this age of Concorde and heart-transplants is 28,000. A hundred years ago it was 30,000 and then, too, it was busier in other ways. The earth below was honeycombed by mine-shafts and the sky-line above punctured by more than fifty mills of the dark, Satanic variety. Its tight little streets were cold and damp, like the soil and the climate, and people took their pleasure wherever they could find it in a town that was Liberal, Nonconformist and sharply divided on the subject of alcohol.

The working men to the east drank heavily and happily, but were opposed, to the last drop and final page of the Bible, by a sober, God-fearing west. On one side of the town there were illicit distilleries cut fifty feet into the valley slopes, reached perilously by crawling through tunnels no bigger around than a man's body; on the other side there was the Temperance Inn, which cheered the soul with coffee and tea.

Darwen's football club had been properly formed only four years before they thumbed their noses at the whole social structure of the game. Their colours were black and white, and they shared their large and carefully manicured ground at Barley Bank, half a mile from the railway station, with the local cricket club.

There were forty-three entrants in the Cup that season and Darwen came through the first round without kicking a ball: their opponents, the Birch club from Manchester, scratched. In the second round they beat neighbouring Eagley by 'four goals and a disputed goal to one', despite playing with only ten men. One of their forwards, Dr J. Gledhill, who lived in Manchester, got off at the wrong station and arrived, breathless and shame-faced, in time to watch the last few minutes of the game.

It was now that Darwen began to appreciate that ambition could be expensive. Most teams of working men in Lancashire did not venture far out of their own parish, often walking to an opponent's ground, but Darwen were about to be invited to leave their familiar backcloth of pitheads and smoking chimneys, and travel south. Darwen were drawn to play the Remnants at Kennington Oval and, with light and teasing snow swirling around them on a bitterly cold day, they won 'a most spiritedly conducted game' by three goals to two, with the winning goal coming in extra time. The round trip, however, cost them a wounding £31 1s 2d, at a time when a man could sail to Australia for fourteen guineas or buy a grand country house in Kent for £800.

This left Darwen critically short of money, and their embarrassment became acute when they learnt they would have to go to London again in the fourth round to play the Old Etonians. They even contemplated scratching but, almost as a last resort, they appealed to the town to help their working lads 'compete against government inspectors, university professors and noblemen's sons'. The town puffed itself up with pride. Work-worn hands were thrust deep into pockets. Collections were made at public houses, in mills and mines, at the local Post Office and branches of the Co-op. Contributions followed from the mayor, aldermen and councillors, solicitors, farmers, butchers, plumbers and manufacturers. The money rolled in: Entwistle and Nutters workmen (15 shillings), the Misses Sutcliffe (5s), Seth Harwood's joiners (10s), a London friend, per Saml. Shorrock (6s), Turncrofts middle pit (8s 6d), Inspector Norris (2s). The early subscriptions were private but then a public 'London fund' was formally established.

Darwen suddenly began to relish their new challenge.

Darwen versus the Old Etonians at the Oval! The town was gripped fast in what was perhaps the first case of that grave derangement known as 'Cup fever'. Darwen was moonstruck.

The Old Etonians belonged to another galaxy: in the nine seasons between 1875 (the fourth year of the Cup) and 1893 they reached the final on six occasions. They were a side of colour and strength, breeding and ability; and no one captured the essence of their quality more than the Honourable (later Lord) Arthur F. Kinnaird.

Here was football's answer to W.G. Grace; perhaps, indeed, Grace was cricket's brave reply to Kinnaird. It could even be argued that Kinnaird did more to popularize football than any man who ever lived. For more than half a century, as player, official and noble head of the establishment, he watched and cherished the game through its most important years of evolution.

Kinnaird's football education began when he entered Eton for the Michaelmas term of 1861 and he continued playing, with huge passion and success, until 1892 and his 45th birthday. He played in nine FA Cup Finals between 1872 and 1883 and finished on the winning side in five of them, three with the Wanderers, two with the Old Etonians. He was president of the Football Association for thirty-three years and president, too, of the YMCA of England and Lord High Commissioner to the General Assembly, Church of Scotland.

The man was exceptional, large, muscular and hearty, a mixture of joy and resolution, warmth and spirit. Even his appearance was a delight. He had a full beard, auburn in colour, and his playing strip never changed: long white flannel ducks, whatever jersey was necessary on his powerful shoulders and, on his high-browed head, a little blue-and-white quartered cricket cap. He played in every position, forward, half-back, back, even goalkeeper, and his style can broadly be described as robust.

This was no staid wearer of coronet and ermine. He relished hacking – defined in the rules as 'kicking an adversary intentionally' – and never flinched a challenge. But there was no malice in his character and he accepted knocks as happily as he gave them. Francis Marindin, captain of the Old Etonians and later president of the FA himself, was to recall with immodest delight his reply to a lament by Kinnaird's mother that 'Arthur is always playing football and will one day surely come home with a broken leg.' 'Pray don't be alarmed,' replied Marindin. 'You may be sure it won't be his.'

Old men with long memories were to claim that Kinnaird would not have been allowed to stay on the field for five minutes in later days, and Kinnaird himself was to write a letter in his winter years in which, with obvious pride, he said he still carried the marks and scars he acquired as a player.

Kinnaird's appetite for football was enormous. He could never understand players who complained that an extra match in mid-week was too great a strain and insisted that he thought nothing of three hard games in a week and of then taking a little exercise in some other form 'just to keep myself fit'. His love for the sport was staunch and unwavering and he once told an audience: 'I believe all right-minded people have good reason to thank God for the great progress of this popular national game.'

His opinion of his own ability was endearingly modest – 'Second to none'. But it was an opinion many shared and certainly there was no one in the game who commanded more affection or whose face was better known. On his way to one Cup Final the crowd even stopped the carriage in which Kinnaird and his family were travelling, took the horses out of the shafts and themselves drew the carriage to the Oval pavilion.

Kinnaird was a measure of the opposition that Darwen were to face. The Old Etonians could also count on such players as Major (later Sir Francis) Marindin himself, who was a goalkeeper of 'rare and inordinate courage', Christian, 'a reliable man who kicks well with either foot', Goodhart, 'a very good forward who dribbles well and unselfishly and is always in front of goal when wanted' and Whitfield, 'a very good wing player who works unceasingly and is much improved in pace'.

The game's laws and methods were still evolving. Shinguards had been introduced in 1874, the crossbar replaced tape a year later, and the referee's whistle was first heard in 1878; but the two-handed throw did not arrive until 1883 and goal-nets and penalty-kicks until 1891. Inclination, too, was swinging slowly from the individual game towards collective team play. Only ten years before, the standard formation had been seven forwards and three defenders, with the emphasis on dribbling. The man in possession held onto the ball as of right: he put his head down, remembered his Queen and country, and burrowed as hard as he could into everything that moved. There was a method of 'backing up' but this was largely to harrass the opposition and fend off would-be challengers. A pass was not expected.

By 1879, however, the style was less primal and Charles Alcock was able to write: 'Skill in dribbling necessitates something more than a go-ahead, fearless, headlong onslaught on the enemy's citadel. It requires a quick eye at discovering a weak point and *nous* to calculate and decide the chances of a successful passage.' Now there were two full-backs, two half-backs and six forwards, of which two played on the right, two in the centre and two on the left. The age of the team game had almost arrived.

It was a formation favoured by the north as well as the south although, before their first meeting, the Old Etonians had little idea of the shape and quality of the team from Darwen. The old boys did not know that Duxbury was a goalkeeper of 'great good style' or that Brindle, the left-back, was 'strong and powerful, kicks well and works hard'. They could not have known that thc two half-backs they were to face were so able – Moorhouse, 'a wonderfully good player who although on the small side excels in fly-kicks with either foot' and Knowles, the captain, 'the most steadfast of men'. And what did Marindin and his team know of the Darwen forwards: Marshall, 'of remarkable speed', Gledhill, 'a good centre when he likes to exert himself', W. Kirkham, who was not a regular but 'always fast and willing', R. Kirkham, no relation, but 'a resolute forward', who combined well with Bury, 'a fine forward who screws in with his left foot in good style, has fair speed and can tackle well'.

The Old Etonians could not possibly have guessed that within two years Brindle and Marshall would both play for England; but they may just have heard a distant whisper about two other members of the Darwen side, Fergie Suter and Jimmy Love. They were two Scots who had played for the Partick club in Glasgow but who had stayed on in Darwen, first

Love, Suter later, after Partick had visited the small Lancashire town.

They are two men who, if history mattered tuppence to the modern player, would be remembered with respect and affection; because here, in all probability, were the game's first two professionals. Darwen always denied that the two Scots were directly paid for their services but, significantly, the club did not deny that the jobs Love and Suter were given locally were much better paid than those they had in Glasgow. This is hardly conclusive, but there is evidence that, soon after their Cup run ended, the Lancashire club played a match 'for the benefit of two Scottish gentlemen who have played with Darwen during the past season.'

It would be difficult to understand why so many other Scottish footballers soon followed Love and Suter to Lancashire if their only reason for moving south was a change of climate. It would be equally difficult to understand why the game's amateur establishment immediately made muddled and unsuccessful efforts to grasp the nettle. There was even a proposal from one of the London clubs, just twenty-four hours before Darwen travelled down for their first game against the Old Etonians, that 'no side which does not consist entirely of amateurs, as defined by the rules to be drawn up by the committee, be entitled to compete in the Challenge Cup competition'. They had not begun to accept that the rising prosperity of Lancashire's industrial towns, plus the growing ambition of their football clubs, would make professionalism inevitable.

Charles Alcock was again among the first to recognize a new and important movement within the game. He wrote: 'There is no use to disguise the speedy approach of a time when the subject of professional footballers will require the earnest attention of those on whom devolves the management of Association Football . . . it will be well for those who have the interest of the game at heart to recognize the existence of a problem which will in all likelihood have to be mastered before very long.' It was not until 1885 that the Football Association formally accepted the inevitable but, in the early months of 1879, Darwen were making history with the first of the hired help.

There was no doubt, either, that Suter and Love were the backbone and spirit of Darwen's team; they gave it an exciting new dimension. Their neat, cool ball-control and studied close-passing set them apart from less sophisticated opposition. Love played on the right of their forward line and, in the earlier rounds, managed a hat-trick against Eagley and then scored their winner in extra-time against the Remnants. Suter was Darwen's right-back but his influence on the team was even greater than Love's. He was a dark, strong-featured man, quick but always composed and more than just a defender. He would have done well a hundred years later. Suter is described, in his own time, as 'a brilliant back, very fast and never misses his kick' and 'not far removed from being the best back in the kingdom, certainly the best in Lancashire; splendid kick with either foot, magnificent tackler and dodger; and can use his head with effect. Is seen to best advantage when playing an uphill game.'

The troubles in Afghanistan were nearing their end early in 1879 but the Zulu war had just started; only two days before Darwen's first game with the Old Etonians, 10,000 troops were ordered to South Africa. In England, a long way from Rorke's Drift and Kabul, it had been a bitterly cold winter. The weather by now was improving a little, the worst of the snow and ice had gone, but Thursday, February 13th, was still a miserable day and the Oval was a place of drips and greyness after prolonged heavy rain. A stiff wind and a sodden, slippery pitch must have filled these two sides with apprehension.

Old Etonians: Major F. Marindin; backs – J.C. Weldon and H.H. Calvert; half-backs – Hon. A.F. Kinnaird and E. Christian; forwards – J.B. Chevallier and H.B. Sedgwick (right), A.G. Bonsor and H.C. Goodhart (centre), and H. Whitfield and R.D. Anderson (left).

Darwen: J. Duxbury; backs – F. Suter and W. Brindle; half-backs – W.H. Moorhouse and J. Knowles; forwards – T. Marshall and J. Love (right), J. Gledhill and W. Kirkham (centre), and T. Bury and R. Kirkham (left).

The Old Etonians won the toss and the right to play with the wind, but both sides had difficulty with their control. The kicking was wild and the ball often sliced into touch. But according to *The Athletic News* (a 'weekly journal of amateur sports', price twopence and published in Manchester), 'Kinnaird's throws were again huge and significant'; and it was from one of these that Whitfield put the Old Boys ahead. Christian added a second a few minutes later, after fine play by Whitfield and Bonsor. Another enormous throw by Kinnaird enabled Goodhart to head in the Old Etonians' third goal and, although Darwen were still playing with heart and intelligence, the London club scored a fourth goal through Goodhart – a header from a corner – before half-time.

Goodhart completed his hat-trick early in the second half – the Old Boys' fifth – and the game seemed irretrievably won and lost. The London team were much bigger, physically, than Darwen and this appeared to be a decisive factor in the demanding conditions. But then came one of the most remarkable turnabouts in the history of the tournament.

Darwen decided they were going to score at least one goal, merely to repair their severely damaged self-respect. The *Darwen News* reported: 'The combined force of Darwen made a grand rush, taking all before them, nor stayed they until they had added honour to their name by breaking through the ranks of their opponents, and finally carried the ball through the posts.'

The team from Lancashire grew stronger, their attacks more persistent; they discovered that although the Old Boys were bigger, they were not, in fact, stronger or fitter. The Old Etonians persisted in long kicking, bull dozing charges and single-minded dribbling and, as the pitch cut up, they began to tire. Darwen made the ball do the work. Their pace was more measured, their variety greater and in the final quarter-hour the balance of power changed dramatically.

Weldon, the Old Etonians' right-back, put the ball into his own net: 5-2. Love, his speed and tenacity now a telling factor, headed powerfully past Major Marindin: 5-3. Again Marindin was beaten, the ball forced through from a scrummage in the Old Etonians' penalty area, involving most of the men on the field. It was 'disallowed' for hands but Darwen protested strongly and the referee changed his mind: 5-4. Then, with minutes left and the tension thick enough to be bottled, Darwen equalized through the lion-hearted Love. The excitement was so intense and sustained that one of the game's two hundred spectators, a native of Swinton, sprained his ankle and broke his umbrella.

Darwen invited the Old Etonians to play extra time – 'to finish it there and then' – but Marindin and his team were exhausted and politely but firmly declined. They generously praised the Lancashire club for their 'pluck, enterprise and liberality,' but refused to change their minds.

> A lot of people are waxing wroth at the Old Etonians (observed *The Athletic News* later) for not agreeing to play an extra 15 or 30 minutes against Darwen. The Etonians were palpably out of condition, and had scarcely a struggle in them when time was called. It would have been downright folly on their part had they agreed to continue the match a little longer, for their opponents were comparatively fresh. The old 'Blues' might just as well have given their Lancashire antagonists the game without playing.
>
> Would Darwen have consented to prolong the game had they been in the Old Etonians' shoes and had just managed to make a draw of it? I am afraid that neither they nor any other club would have consented to such a one-sided proposition. Of course, it is very hard lines for the Darwenites that they are thus obliged to make an extra journey to London, but when they entered into the competition they had their eyes fully open to the conditions, and as the rules regulating the contest have been strictly adhered to, no-one is to blame; it is simply a matter of ill-luck.

So Darwen returned to Lancashire to worry again about the cost of another trip to London. By now, however, the town believed their team capable of anything; the enthusiasm reached such a peak that one writer in the *Darwen Times* complained bitterly of 'football-mania' and wondered what would become of it. The correspondent added that he had seen clubs playing on Sundays when 'their oaths would have stamped the lowest beer-shop with disgrace'. But the rest of the town happily rallied again. The 'London fund' continued to swell. One benefactor, Chas. P. Huntington Esq. J.P., even promised after the first game against the Old Etonians 'that whatever the subsequent cost, or however many journeys the team were under the necessity of making' he would stand one-third of the expense himself. His contribution in the end came to £19.

Even more remarkably, ten pounds were donated by the Football Association and another five pounds by the Old Etonians themselves. As Sir Frederick Wall, secretary of the Football Association from 1895 to 1934, was to write in later years: 'Let me ask you, can you imagine a crack professional club in these days giving any money to a Third Division team for the coming struggle between them?'

Perhaps the consciences of the Establishment had been troubled by a trenchant article in another sporting paper, the *Athletic World*. It observed:

> The rules under which the Association Challenge Cup is contested should certainly be very much modified. As the regulations at present stand, the Londoners, or clubs in and about the metropolis, are favoured at the expense of the provincial brethren. If the affair is to be made a national competition, the proviso about playing the last three rounds of ties at Kennington Oval must certainly be rescinded. If I understand the thing correctly, the Surrey club benefits materially by the matches being played on their ground. But whilst this arrangement may be a comfortable one for London clubs, a great and glaring injustice is perpetrated upon those to be found in the country . . . I venture to think that if this law about the last three ties being played at Kennington Oval was done away with, twice the number of entries would be secured, and the contest become so much more additionally interesting.

Darwen were again, albeit unwillingly, helping to shape the future of the game. The following year the FA grouped entries for the Cup in regional divisions to save money and time.

A crowd of three hundred were at the local station to cheer Darwen away on the 12.27 on Friday, March 7th. The Great Northern Company provided a 'first-class third carriage', padded and cushioned, and one onlooker supposed the 'Darruners' would have no objection if they could always travel in such comfort.

The weather had changed for the better by now, and the start of the first replay twenty-four hours later was watched by a large crowd, as Darwen kicked off at fourteen minutes past two with the gasometer behind them and a glaring sun shining into their faces. Darwen were unchanged, but the Old Etonians were strengthened by the return of L. Bury, an England international, who replaced H.H. Calvert at left-back, while in attack C.J. Clarke and J.R. Sturgis were preferred to Bonsor and Anderson. One of the Old Boys' team travelled from Paris to play, while Major Marindin journeyed down from Inverness. No chances were taken, no excuses accepted. This was a match to win.

Darwen's own sporting paper, the *East Lancashire Cricket and Football Times,* was printed for the first time that same week; its birth and the success of the town's football club were no coincidence. On various days the paper carried four reports of the second drawn game between Darwen and the Old Etonians, one by 'a Manchester critic' who wrote:

> W. Kirkham set the globe rolling and the play was at once lively. The Etonian forwards were in fine form, with good pace, close dribbling and dodging; Whitfield especially worked well, and he was rewarded with a goal.
>
> It was evident the Etonians were 50 per cent better in passing and endurance than on the last occasion. Some gallant efforts were now made by the Lancashire men to score, and the attack and defence of both sides in turn were deservedly recognized by the anxious spectators. Hard luck fell to both sides, and a goal might have been scored for Darwen had not two players missed the kick. The ball was then taken towards the Darwen goal, but it was returned and seen bounding from head to head in the mouth of the Etonian goal. At length the defenders cleared the goal. The leather was pursued by the Etonians and Gledhill, when the latter by an unexpected manoeuvre stopped the ball, wheeled round and sent it to the goal, where Bury and Kirkham gave the finishing touch. Thus even the contestants played with vigour until half-time.
>
> The game was resumed more keenly than ever. Sedgwick and Clarke were repeatedly cheered for fine plucky play, whilst Suter bewildered a host of forwards, much to the enjoyment of the eager crowd. The Etonians were again the

first to score. The back-play was perhaps the strongest ever shown by two English clubs, tackling and fly-kicks being much noticed; in fact, the forwards had much trouble in reaching and nursing the ball. W. Kirkham robbed Christian of some fine kicks by rushing up and placing his foot as an obstruction, whilst the left-wing at length non-plussed the elected international back (L. Bury) by some good dribbling, which ultimately secured the Darwenites a goal. Love unfortunately received a kick from Kinnaird which interfered with his co-operation as Marshall's partner . . . the game continued on to the end of 1½ hour when, no score resulting, an extra half hour was played which also was of no avail.'

The final score: 2-2. Scorers: Old Etonians – Clarke and Whitfield, Darwen – R. Kirkham and T. Bury.

A second replay and yet another journey to London was necessary; and now the *Cricket and Football Times* had this to say: 'We speak plain when we say the Darwen team are completely tired of this 220 mile journey before engaging in a keen and trying conflict. They wish they had not to go again, but seeing they have come off so well, the gentry and people of Darwen all say they must go on until they are beaten or bring back the Cup. In future years, no one need look for Darwen entering (even if they should be successful) except some of the matches may be played away from the City. Considering that they have gone so far, they will not now give up until they either win or lose.'

Nottingham Forest, meanwhile, were waiting to play the winners, and the *Nottingham Journal* entered the fray: 'The Northerners are not very popular in London. Many of them I am told, are 'sons of the soil' and they carry about with them unmistakable evidences of their paternity, whilst – if imprecautions upon the most beautiful of human features were availing – there is scarcely a member of the Etonian team who would not at this moment be totally blind. If, in their next essay, Darwen should beat their more aristocratic opponents, they will scarcely find the "rushing about" tactics pay against the Reds.'

Letters continued to reach the offices of the *Cricket and Football Times*. One counselled the Darwen team 'to be careful to get a very good night's rest, and before going onto the field to have so lined their inner-man as to be well able to stand the heavy charges of the heavy team.' Even the 'Lancashire witches' were called upon 'to direct the ball between one or other of the citadels the moment before the referee calls time; what a lot of money it would save Darwen and what anxiety it would remove from the breasts of the collegians.'

The third game took place on March 15th, with Darwen obliged to play McLachlan instead of W. Kirkham (who had injured a foot) as one of their centre-forwards. The team as a whole was feeling weary and probably resigned to playing the Old Etonians once a week for the rest of their days. The spirit was willing, however, and for quarter of an hour they even had the better of things. But, with a strong wind cutting across a bone-dry pitch and Darwen's captain, Knowles, limping slightly after a knock, the Old Boys slowly took control. They were more durable, they had whatever luck was going and in front of goal they were certainly more effective. The final score, 6-2, faithfully reflected the shape of the game.

'The Comparison is now before the public', said the *Cricket and Football Times,* 'and it is for the latter to say whether Darwen have been pursuing a foolish and empty phantom, or that they have gallantly endeavoured to lay before the football world that there is some cause to treasure up ambition in their hearts.'

Properly, too, the *Cricket and Football Times* offered its own opinion, which nicely reflected what most 'Darruners' were thinking: 'Darwen has done more than any club from the North of England has done before . . . they have made themselves a name, not simply in Lancashire but in every county in England.' This much said, the *C. and F. T.* died peacefully after just thirteen issues.

Darwen, to their own considerable surprise, contributions having 'far exceeded the expectations of the most sanguine', were to finish with an overall profit after their four expeditions to London. Income: £175 14s 4½d. Expenditure: £118 17s. Profit: £56 17s 4½d. Result: happiness. Mr Micawber would have approved.

The Old Etonians beat Nottingham Forest 2-1 in the semi-finals – a game that was 'fast and well contested on a terribly unpleasant and trying afternoon' – before going on to beat Clapham Rovers 1-0 in the final. Darwen, having presented the Old Boys with their toughest obstacle, immediately and easily convinced themselves that they were 'second in England under Association Rules'.

Fergie Suter, Darwen's inspiration, was to make his mark again and again in the Cup. He joined Blackburn Rovers two years later and did much to establish their place in history: he helped them win the trophy three years in succession (1884-6), with Major Marindin the referee on each occasion. Suter continued to live in Darwen, however, and later became a prominent man in the town, the licensee of the Millstone Hotel and then the White Lion, before retiring to Blackpool where he died. Poor Jimmy Love was less fortunate: he was killed during the bombardment of Alexandria in 1882.

Darwen were one of the original applicants for admission to the Football League when it was formed in 1888. They failed to gain entry by a single vote; but three seasons later the League increased its number from twelve to fourteen, and Darwen and Stoke City were elected. Darwen finished bottom and, with the introduction of a Second Division in 1892-3, they were relegated. They immediately won promotion, however, but were relegated again the following season and then spent five undistinguished years in Division Two before, short of money again, they slipped quietly out of a competition which was becoming increasingly dominated by bigger clubs from more heavily populated areas. A year later, in 1900, Darwen left their ground at Barley Bank. Now, on the site, there is a school and tidy rows of terraced houses with coloured-glass windows and neat stone walls.

Twice more, though, Darwen were to be beckoned by history. They reached the semi-finals in 1881, when they were beaten 4-1 by the Old Carthusians, and in 1931-2, then the champions of the Lancashire Combination, they were drawn to play Arsenal at Highbury in the third round – the Arsenal of Herbert Chapman, who were to finish runners-up in the League that season and to be champions for the next three years.

A souvenir programme, published locally in Darwen, did justice to the occasion:

> History repeats itself! Darwen again challenges the Metropolis. From Darwen went the first Northern team to challenge the South in the English Cup competition . . . on January 9th, 1932, Darwen will challenge the Arsenal's Big Guns at Highbury in the same competition. Darwen has many claims to fame. It was the first town in the Provinces to house the notorious Gandhi; was the cock-pit of the General Election; and now Darwen has its eye on the spoils of the great Soccer knock-out. What Darwen is thinking: can these boys from Lancashire's mills and workshops put out the £40,000 Highbury Battery? Goliath fell! Rome fell! It may be the great Arsenal will fall!!!

Arsenal, alas, had no sense of history. They won 11-1.

2 Tottenham...1901

Quiz-masters have always had a soft spot for Tottenham Hotspur. Those sovereign founts of all knowledge never tire of asking for the name of the only non-League club to have won the FA Cup since the formation of the Football League in 1888.

It is a question with which the future will never tamper. Spurs were a Southern League club when they won the tournament in brilliant fashion in 1901, and it is as certain as anything can be in football that no club outside the League will ever repeat the feat. As Sam Goldwyn would have observed, this is now an achievement which is, 'in two words: im-possible'.

Spurs' final triumph over Sheffield United gave the game in London fresh status and new impetus at a time when the north and midlands seemed bent on making it as much their own property as Rugby League is today. The south had kept an aristocratic hand on the Cup for the first ten years of its life, but Blackburn Olympic beat the Old Etonians in the 1883 final and the golden age of the amateur was over. 'It'll have a good home', said S.A. Warburton, the Olympic captain, as he held the Cup aloft back in Blackburn, 'and it'll ne'er go back to Lon'on.' He was right in one sense: the original trophy was stolen from a Birmingham shop window one September night in 1895 and was never recovered. For a long time, too, his boast held good in the sense in which he meant it.

Between the Olympic's victory over Kinnaird's Old Etonians and Spurs' wholly unexpected triumph in the year of Queen Victoria's death – a period of eighteen years – the Cup was never once allowed to find a home south of Birmingham. It was also strictly the preserve of the League clubs – a League which by 1901, its thirteenth season, consisted of two divisions of eighteen clubs with Arsenal, and Arsenal alone, carrying the colours of the south.

Spurs were younger than the FA Cup itself. According to a story which only the soulless will challenge, they were formed in

1882 under a lamp-post in Tottenham High Street, the second on the right along the High Road towards Bruce Grove. Their name had its source in local history: it was here that the Northumberland family owned great estates and what better figurehead than the most celebrated member of the House of Percy, Harry Hotspur, whose heroics even caught the fancy of Shakespeare – 'Gallant Hotspur . . . theme of honour's tongue.'

They played their first games on the local marshes, between the railway and the River Lea, but later hired a pitch behind a nursery in Northumberland Park, a private ground which enabled them to charge admission money. Spurs were now a club in a hurry. They competed in the London Association Cup, the London Senior Cup, in which they were immediately beaten 8-2 by the Old Etonians, the Southern Alliance, which gave them an exciting early taste of league football, and then the FA Amateur Cup, which was the south's answer to the northern monopoly of the FA Cup.

Spurs turned professional on the Monday before Christmas in 1895 and, the following season, a mark of their fast rising reputation, they were admitted to the First Division of the Southern League. They finished fourth in their first season, third in their second and in 1899-1900 they won the championship with basically the side that was going to win the FA Cup. That same championship season they moved to White Hart Lane behind the White Hart pub in Tottenham High Street – the brewers who owned the land were warmed by the idea of instant custom – and their first groundsman was John Over, the man who had marked out the Oval when the first Test match was played there, against Australia, in 1880. Over's pitch at White Hart Lane was smooth and rich and soon recognized as one of the best in the land. It was at this time, too, that Tottenham at last settled on the colours they wanted to wear. They had begun with an all navy-blue strip but often played in white, switched to blue-and-white halves, then to red shirts with blue shorts, next to chocolate and gold and, finally and happily, to white shirts and navy blue shorts.

Tottenham's most important decision as the new century approached, however, was to take John Cameron onto their pay-roll. He, more than anyone, shaped and nurtured the side which was to inspire a local bard to write:

In the Games Olympian
  There were heroes, there were men
As we learn in classics lay –
  Not more brave than you today,
Not more worthy of renown,
  Not more fit to wear the crown,
Hands of fair ones in their bowers,
  Made for them with Myrtle flowers,
Winners of the Cup at last,
  Like those heroes of the past,
Ringing, heartie, bonnie Spurs.

Cameron joined Spurs in the late summer of 1898 and, as player-manager-secretary, he had a say in the club's every thought and decision. He had played for Queen's Park and Everton, and was an engaging, rather precise man who thought before he spoke and then thought some more before he acted. He was perceptive, conscientious and a worker: a knowledgeable secretary and also the first secretary of the Professional Football Players' Union, an ambitious manager who understood people and an inside-forward in the classic Scottish style. He was nearly six feet tall, slim but well muscled and a man who kept cool in moments of tension or crisis. He liked the ball on the ground, his passes intelligently directed and nicely weighted, and he had an instinctive relationship with the players around him. He was a natural footballer and he knew exactly the kind of men he wanted in his team.

He disliked 'rough play and rough manners' and believed that to become a professional footballer 'you must have exceptional qualities of a personal character . . . education makes all the difference'. Here, perhaps, was the father of Spurs' great tradition for elegance and style. Down through the twentieth century, in lean years as well as fat, the club has held firm to a belief that football is something more than merely muscle and sweat. The name of Tottenham Hotspur is identified with quality; and John Cameron was the man who set the standard. He chose his players with great care and, in a remarkably short time, gathered together a team which blended experience with ambition, skill with courage, and speed with vision.

Cameron took George Clawley from Stoke to be his goalkeeper, a first-class technician with dependable hands and more courage than was good for him. Ted Hughes, at centre-half, was a man Cameron had admired at Everton, a Welsh international who at five feet six inches was the shortest member of the side. What he lacked in height, however, he more than compensated for with his anticipation, speed off the mark and bounce off the ground. Many were convinced he had a plate of steel set into his forehead; his heading was prodigious, as long and hard as many a man's kick.

The full-backs, Sandy Tait and Harry 'Tiger' Erentz, were an oddly contrasting pair. Tait, on the left, was regarded as one of the best full-backs in the English game. He came from Preston and was a dour, dark, heavy-browed Scot who took himself and his football very seriously. Off the field he was lost in a crowd; on the field he was a fierce, unyielding competitor, a man whose modest frame seemed to light up with energy. He shadowed opponents remorselessly and tackled with swallow-swift certainty. North London had a name for him: Terrible Tait. Erentz, on the right, was another Scot but a strong, solid and happy man, a reliable team-mate and good friend. But he, too, was a formidable opponent, difficult to go round or over and impossible to run through. He conceded nothing to any man.

Tom Morris, the right-half, came from Gainsborough, strong, cool, tireless and not blessed with an outsize conscience. Here was the hard man of the side and a perfect foil for Jack Jones at left-half. Jones, a Welsh international, was a natural leader who got on well with Cameron; and Cameron, despite his own influential presence in the side, was astute enough to leave the captaincy with Jones. The Welshman was a skilful and aggressive player who read the game well. He was sensitive to its changing moods and patterns, and always ready to link up with his forwards. He was the man, more than any, who turned the screw when opponents began to wilt, but he was also always prepared to pull his weight in defence.

Tom Smith, the outside-right, was another recruit from Preston, a fast, single minded player, a former sprint-champion who – in running shoes or football boots – always went hard and straight for the finishing line. Cameron himself slotted in at inside-right, relishing Smith's speed outside him but always aware that it was his centre-forward, another Scot and another former Preston player, who was most likely to put the ball into the net. The centre-forward was Alexander (Sandy) Brown, who was no stylist or architect but had that simple and priceless gift of being able to score goals. Brown was open-faced and uncomplicated, not a footballer in the sense that Cameron and Jones were but a devil in the air, two-footed, courageous and guided by an extra-sensory instinct for knowing when and where to go inside an opponent's penalty area. It is a quality which cannot be taught or copied; it is God-given, and it defies analysis. Brown was to hit fifteen of the twenty goals Spurs scored in their Cup triumph, scoring in every round, an achievement which has not been bettered in a hundred years.

Spurs' inside-left, completing an all-Scottish inside trio, was Davie Copeland from Ayr, a player's player who made others look better, a man who covered and harassed, who drew defenders and left space for colleagues to exploit. He was a support-player and happy with his role, a very different kind of being from Jack Kirwan on the left-wing, a Dubliner who had played with Cameron at Everton. Kirwan was an Irish international and a player of infinite variety. He could make defenders wonder if they had missed their proper vocation. Kirwan and Copeland complemented each other beautifully.

They were eleven players who became a good side almost immediately and an outstanding one very quickly; but it must be admitted that their success was at least shared by the north. Spurs may have been a London club but Cameron had cast his net wide. Their team included five Scots, two Welshmen, an Irishman and three Englishmen from the top-side of the Trent. It must be conceded, too, that a team of such wit and substance hardly fits comfortably into the role of giant killers. But they were outside the Football League which, certainly in the north, was considered to embrace all the clubs of any worth in the country. Before more than one of Spurs' Cup-ties that season, the newspapers had talked patronizingly about 'Jack and his master' — and Jack, undoubtedly, was always Tottenham. Cameron himself admitted that southern football occupied 'a peculiar and lonely position in the football world'. Another Southern League club, Southampton, had reached the final in 1900 but they had been soundly spanked by Bury by four goals to nil. Two years later Southampton reached the final once more, but again they were beaten, this time by Sheffield United. The renaissance of the south had begun, however, and Spurs were about to lead the way.

It cannot be claimed, either, that Spurs' road to the final was strewn with rose petals. They won the Cup the hard way. In the first round Spurs were drawn at home with Preston North End, who were a First Division club though not the force of a decade before. In 1888-9 Preston had won the first League championship without losing a match and the FA Cup without conceding a goal. They were known, affectionately, as 'the old Invincibles'. They were champions again the following season and runners-up for the next three. In 1900, moreover, they had knocked Spurs out of the Cup in the first round, by a goal to nil, and there was little in the stars to suggest the outcome this time would be very different.

Preston scored first and although Spurs gradually took control they were frustrated by Peter McBride, the Lancashire club's goalkeeper, who was gloriously inspired. He had one of those days when the ball seemed to look for him, and with little more than eight minutes left Spurs appeared to be on their way out of the tournament. But then Kirwan, with a wiggle and a change of pace, got away on the left and his centre found Brown who had been only a timid shadow of his real self. This time, however, Brown reached a ball that seemed beyond him and his firm, true header earned Spurs a replay. Preston, with home advantage now theirs, were firmer favourites than ever; but four days later they found themselves out-manoeuvred and out-gunned. Spurs were three up at half-time and winners by 4-2, with Brown contributing a hat-trick. Brown, remember, had played for Preston for three years. He left the Deepdale pitch a happy and contented man.

The second round presented Spurs with an even bigger hurdle, Bury, the Cup-holders themselves, and for the first quarter of the tie at White Hart Lane the Southern League club were in mortal danger of being overrun. Bury took the lead after only two minutes, and their game had an edge to it which caused Spurs enormous problems. In the thirtieth minute, though, Spurs made a rare and desperate attack and Brown, always Brown, whipped in a shot which the Bury goalkeeper touched but could not stop. It gave Spurs the confidence their game had lacked, and early in the second half Brown scored again. It was the winner: Bury, try as they did to hold onto the Cup, finished well beaten.

Spurs' third-round opponents held no fear or mystery for them: but Reading, also a Southern League club, had a good, doughty side and, always significantly, they were at home. Reading took an early lead and their strength and resolution disconcerted Spurs although Kirwan still managed to equalize before half-time, against the run of play. Spurs improved after half-time but whether they deserved their replay is questionable: Tait clearly fisted a Reading shot off the line and the referee awarded a goal-kick! The second game at White Hart Lane four days later, however, was very different. Brown was back at his best and scored two of Spurs' three goals. Cameron and his team played some delightful football.

There should have been no doubts anywhere now about Spurs' quality, but if any lingered they were to be dispelled once and for all in their Easter Monday semi-final against West Bromwich Albion at Villa Park. Albion finished bottom of the First Division that season but they had already established themselves as a formidable Cup-team, having reached the final on five occasions and twice finishing winners. But Spurs cared little for such facts. They won by four second-half goals to nil, Brown scoring all of them, of which the third was the best, a low, venemous shot from nearly thirty yards. As the *Sporting Life* observed, 'Spurs had eleven men who all pulled one way.'

Spurs had to wait a few days more to discover who they would play in the final. Sheffield United and Aston Villa had drawn their semi-final at Nottingham, but in the replay at Derby the Sheffield club played with style and verve to win by 3-0. United were a First Division club of high renown, having finished runners-up to Aston Villa the previous season, and they were immediately made favourites. They had nine full internationals in their side and had beaten four other First Division clubs,

Sunderland, Everton, Wolverhampton Wanderers and Villa on their road to the final, scoring 13 goals against 3. The Cup, as everyone knew, was the property of the north and midlands: Sheffield United were simply its latest guardians.

United were a side of experience, quality and substance – above all, perhaps, substance. Their goalkeeper was Billy 'Fatty' Foulke, who, at 6ft 2ins and 22 stone, was described in his time as 'one of the curiosities of football . . . a wonder to everyone who visits the classic grounds of the game'. His towering, barrel-like figure filled his goal area and, when team pictures were taken, colleagues complained he kept them in shadow. He could send a goal-kick almost into the opposition penalty area and punch the ball to the half-way line. He once swung on his cross bar and snapped it and, more than once, he dangled an irritating opponent by the ankles. Foulke was, however, remarkably nimble, with a good enough technique to play for England. He excelled at saving penalties and such was his girth that opponents were known to admit they sometimes shot for his stomach, trying to bury the ball, rather than keep it low, the kind of shot to which he was most vulnerable. Foulke was a huge, loveable eccentric who once declared: 'I don't mind what you call me so long as you don't call me late for lunch.'

Foulke weighed almost as much as his two full-backs put together, Harry Thickett, another English international and one of the most reliable backs of his time, and Peter Boyle, a robust Irishman who had been bought from Sunderland – again an international. Foulke, Thickett and Boyle were a celebrated combination, a team within a team.

United's half-back line consisted of three more English internationals. W.H. Johnson, on the right, was a consistent and polished player, a Yorkshireman who made the game look easy; Tommy Morren, at centre-half, came from Middlesborough, a pillar of the side, a small, wiry man whose judgement was impeccable and whose temperament was cool and even; and at left-half there was, above all, Ernest Needham. He *was* United, their captain and inspiration, a living, breathing definition of the phrase 'perpetual motion'. He was known as 'Nudger', a stubborn, awkward player when he was defending, a man of speed and huge enterprise when pushing forward. 'Neither height nor weight is an essential qualification for a half-back', he was to write later, 'for it is well known that some players have been internationals who have not scaled 10-5 nor reached a greater height than 5-5.' Here, exactly, were his own measurements. 'The work of a half-back is considered the most onerous on the field of play, and having had a long experience in this line of work I am not disposed to disagree with the conclusions arrived at by the unanimous opinion of experts.' Needham was happily known as 'the prince of half-backs'. He was one of the great men of his time.

The attack was an interesting mix. Walter Bennett on the right-wing was a crowd pleaser, a little man with fine, tight control and a big shot. 'Rather erratic' it was written of him, 'but when serious a thorn in the side of backs. Still, hardly the sort of player to rely on for any one particular match.' Charlie Field, at inside-right, was on the light side but a fighter, a forager and a busy provider. G.A. Hedley was considered one of the best centre-forwards of his day, and while one contemporary critic noted his 'tendency to turn in the direction of his own goal when trying to circumvent an opponent', he was better known for his ability to shoot hard and low from all angles and the intelligent way in which he fed his wings. Fred Priest, at inside-left, was an individualist full of feints and sleights of foot, who could 'plough his way through opponents in exciting style', while outside him, on the left-wing, was H.B. Lipsham, who had come from Crewe and was speedy, fearless and a good tackler. Bennett, Hedley and Priest were English internationals, Field and Lipsham the only men in the side who had not won representative honours. Field, too, was the only southerner in the side . . . the only southerner to play in the 1901 final.

The day of the final – Saturday, April 20th – was perfect. A day stolen from high summer. The sky was cloudless, apart from an odd little ball of cottonwool, and a warm sun combined sublimely with the gentlest of breezes. Sheffield United's support, 40,000 and more, rolled into town by train. Drags, brakes and carriages rumbled over London Bridge towards Sydenham and the Crystal Palace. Local railway stations blinked and surrendered: the crush was so great that doors folded and windows were smashed. Thousands were at the

Palace by half-past ten. They were wise, because Tottenham's supporters, from Seven Sisters and Bruce Grove and a score of other rendezvous, were now approaching the ground by way of Denmark Hill. Charabancs, nose to tail, decked in blue and white, edged their way slowly into the confusion. North and South fused into a new community.

The scene outside the Crystal Palace looked like a battlefield; the walks, roads and open spaces outside this great saucer of a ground, the second famous home of the Cup Final, were black with jostling humanity. Inside history was assembling . . . the biggest crowd ever gathered to watch a football match. It was a magnificently colourful sight. White handkerchiefs were tied over heads, and caps and bonnets pulled low as protection against the sun. The crowd, observed the *Tottenham Weekly Herald,* looked like 'a forest of trees covered with pink and white blossom'. Tall trees outside the ground offered hundreds more a free spectacle, uncomfortable and dangerous perhaps but the risks were happily accepted. The Spurs were playing the Cutlers but, no less importantly, the south was challenging the north. There was a huge sense of occasion about this day.

The first attendance figure given was 114,815, but this was later amended to 110,820. No matter: it dwarfed the previous best of 73,833 (for the 1899 final between Sheffield United and Derby County) and was a world record which stood until 1913, when Aston Villa and Sunderland attracted a crowd of 120,081. The caterers, it seemed, were not surprised. Provisions laid on included 2,500 sandwich loaves, each weighing 8 lbs and capable of making 36 sandwiches; 1,000 bread and butter loaves, each weighing 5 lbs; 1,000 household loaves; 21,000 rolls; 45,120 portions of best cake; 16,000 portions of lunch cake; 20,000 French pastries; 24,000 scones; 10,000 bath buns; 10,000 plain buns; 200 rumps of steak, each capable of producing 26 steaks; 40 whole lambs; 60 fore-ribs of beef, each weighing 40 lbs; 22,400 lbs of potatoes; 400 fowls; 200 ducks; 1,728 gallons of milk; 120,000 bottles of mineral water; and much, much more. The mind and stomach can only wonder! Was all this food sold? How and where did they cook the meat and fowl? Who prepared the bread, rolls, scones and vegetables? Where did they eat? And how much time was left for actually watching the match?

There was a moment or two of low drama, or perhaps slightly higher comedy, when Spurs arrived at the Palace. They could not get near the main entrance because of the crush, so Ralph Bullock, the director in charge of the party, led them all around to a small, closely-guarded private entrance a couple of hundred yards away and passed through a message requesting entry. Long minutes later they had their reply from an FA official: 'You must enter by the gate shown on your ticket.' Bullock's second message was tersely to the point: 'We cannot get in at the main entrance because of the crowd. Our non-appearance will be your responsibility.' A puffing official appeared immediately. Spurs were in.

Tottenham's players, nonetheless, were clearly in good spirits when they took the field before the kick-off at half-past three, and there was no doubt their supporters had a noticeable edge in number and volume. The two teams lined up like this: *Tottenham:* Clawley; Erentz, Tait; Morris, Hughes, Jones; Smith, Cameron, Brown, Copeland, Kirwan. *Sheffield United:* Foulke; Thickett, Boyle; Johnson, Morren, Needham; Bennett, Field, Hedley, Priest, Lipsham. The referee, who was to prove a central figure in the drama to come, was Mr Arthur Kingscott of Derby.

The *Tottenham Weekly Herald,* with clear eye, sturdy phrase and no more bias than it was entitled to, saw the game like this:

> On the whole the football which the match produced was of good quality – better than has been seen in many finals. It was not a real tip-top exhibition, but allowing for all the circumstances which must be taken into consideration in a fixture of such vital importance it was quite equal to expectations. The sides were well matched, which was somewhat contrary to the opinions of most Sheffielders, many of whom seemed to think they only had to come to London to 'lift' the Cup. There was no doubt a deal of cocksuredness about the North country folk. One found it in the confident manner in which they spoke, and in the remarks which appeared in their newspapers. But before the match was over they had reason to realise that self complacency was scarcely the most suitable frame of mind.

The bones of the game were that Sheffield United took the lead after only ten minutes, Priest running smoothly into a pass from Field before hitting the ball past the unsighted Clawley from eighteen yards. Spurs kept cool, however, and a quarter of an hour later a long free-kick gave Brown the chance to equalize with a header and complete his record of having scored in every round of the Cup. 'It was a scene for the biograph operator', exclaimed the *Weekly Herald*. 'The tangled mass of humanity vibrated with delight.'

Five minutes after the start of the second half, the sun now behind Spurs, there were even greater vibrations. Tottenham took the lead with a goal that was finely made and robustly taken. Jones, Kirwan and Brown moved the ball sweetly from centre-midfield to Cameron on the right, who made ground, paused, feinted to go right and then, with the United defence in two minds, pushed it back inside to Brown again. The centre-forward was under pressure but he got his shot in with minimum wind-up and the ball cannoned into the net off the underside of the bar. Surely now, and the conviction was there in the soul-stirring thunder of the cheers which rolled out over the capital city, it was Tottenham's Cup.

The Cup, however, does not like itself to be taken for granted. It was going to be Spurs' year; but not yet. Two minutes after Brown had put the London club in front, United equalized with a goal that was to be argued about for the next fifty years.

Lipsham broke away along the Sheffield left and drove in a shot that Clawley, who had left his line, got his hands to but then dropped behind him. Bennett darted in to challenge Clawley, recovering quickly, pushed the ball outside the post and the near linesman immediately signalled a corner. Referee Kingscott now arrived on the scene and appeared to be waving aside his linesman's decision. Clawley, relieved, placed the ball for a goal-kick. But, to a rumble of disbelief which swelled into a huge roar of southern anger and northern elation, the referee solemnly turned and pointed to the centre spot. He was giving United a goal! He was convinced that when Clawley dropped Bennett's shot behind him, the ball had crossed the line.

The Tottenham supporters did not let Mr Kingscott off the

hook. They kept up a running commentary that was rustically to the point, on his looks, walk, mannerisms and parentage. Every shot was accompanied by derisive shouts of 'Goal'. The rest of the game did not seem to matter. The issue for that day had been settled. A replay was necessary.

The inquest on United's goal dominated the reports on the match. The *Tottenham Weekly Herald* was again commendably fair:

> Personally, we could not say whether the ball went over the line or not – nobody in the Press seats could have been in a position to give a decision. But we have spoken to people who were on a level with the goal-line and who most emphatically declare that the ball was within a foot or a foot and a half of goal. Clawley is very positive that he stopped it in time and Tait, who was almost on top of him, says the same . . . it must be said that the referee appeared to have no shadow of a doubt himself that a goal was scored . . . we were rather astonished at what we might almost term his precipitancy. He was not within yards of the goal and that being the case it was remarkable that he did not consult his linesmen, one of whom at any rate was further up the field than he was. Still, we would not say that Mr Kingscott refereed unfairly; his decisions were no doubt given to the best of his belief. Local prejudices no doubt magnify seeming errors and we would not pay attention to all that has been said in his disfavour.

The rest of the newspapers lined up to have their say. 'Linesman' in *The Morning Leader* wrote: 'Of the many competent judges to whom I spoke there was not one to support Mr Kingscott's view. Robert Howie, the well-known London Caledonian forward, assured me that from his position near the goal the ball was never over the line, and apart from the disinterested criticism of outsiders Clawley declared bitterly that it was dead robbery.' 'Rover' in *The Morning Leader* insisted: 'I contend that from the position in which Mr Kingscott stood – facing the goal some 20 yards out – it was a physical impossibility for him to have told whether the ball was over the line or not.' 'Wanderer' in *The Sportsman* wrote: 'Onlookers, whose integrity and impartiality I have no reason to doubt, and who were in a good position for seeing, say that Clawley was about eighteen inches outside the line.' Naturally, too, there was a Sheffield point of view. The *Sheffield Daily Telegraph* said: 'I have it on the authority of a very well-known official of a Nottingham club who was well-placed to see, that the ball was a clear foot over the line at the time Clawley handled it. Few people could be found who took exception of Mr Kingscott's rulings, save those who were blinded by their prejudice and inspired by partisanship.' But, as 'Nemo' summed up sagely in *The Athletic News,* it was a goal 'that will always remain a matter of doubt'.

There was another lighter moment of doubt during the match. The chairmen of the two clubs, Charles Roberts of Tottenham and Charles Stokes of United, sat next to each other, ignorant of each other's identity. Stokes began predicting victory for his own team, although generously applauding the skill of Spurs. Towards the end of the game Frederick Wall, the secretary of the FA, came up and spoke briefly to them both – and still they did not catch on. Wall moved away and then, as an afterthought, called back to Roberts: 'If Spurs win you must make a speech . . . ' Stokes turned to his neighbour: 'What's that he says?' Roberts repeated the instructions and added: 'That's Wall of the FA.' 'Yes, I know that', replied the puzzled Stokes, 'but who the Dickens are you?'

The date for the replay had already been settled: it was to be the following Saturday. It had been decided, too, that Goodison Park, the home of Everton, would be the venue. But Liverpool had protested by letter that a counter-attraction of such importance would seriously affect the gate for their home game with Nottingham Forest the same day and so, immediately after the draw at the Palace, FA councillors and officials met in the pavilion to decide on a new setting. Spurs and Sheffield United both suggested Villa Park, but – for reasons not recorded in the minutes and records of the FA – the replay was given to Burnden Park at Bolton.

It was a curious decision because Bolton's railway station was being extensively altered and the rail company refused to issue cheap excursion tickets for supporters travelling from London and Yorkshire. Nonetheless, there was talk of a 'mighty crowd in which spectators might be crushed' and it was decided that three hundred foot and mounted policemen and twenty firemen with hydrants and hoses should be standing by . . . a wild piece of extravagance because on a day of early wind and rain only 19,905 spectators paid for admission. The full attendance was 22,000, which meant the ground was only half-full.

Spurs spent most of the week at Southport, in a hotel overlooking the sea and run by Sam Redfern, the old music-hall star, and when they arrived at Burnden Park they had the relaxed look of men who knew they were equal to their task. United were still 6 to 4 favourites, however, despite a lingering doubt about the fitness of Ernest Needham which was not cleared until the eleventh hour. Lord Kinnaird was in the crowd, both teams were unchanged and Mr Kingscott was again the referee.

This time there was no honourable basis for argument. The better team won, and that team was Tottenham. Priest put Sheffield United ahead five minutes before half-time, against the run of play, but after the interval the Spurs were at their best, all harmony and variation, and Cameron, Smith and Brown (his fifteenth of the Cup run) scored the goals which returned the Cup to the south.

Now, at last, 'Arbee' of the *Tottenham Weekly Herald* felt entitled to let himself go:

> There are times in a man's life when he thinks a lot of things he can't give expression to, and that's just how I feel about last Saturday's magnificent accomplishment at Bolton. It really seems a hopeless task to adequately paint the picture in the way I would wish the Spurs supporters to read, mark and learn . . . Every man was at his best. No one worked for his own hand. They were simply one magnificent piece of machinery. At every branch of the game they were artists, and none but themselves can ever be their equal.
>
> The first twenty minutes was a marvellous vision for the North Countrymen as the Spurs simply made rings round United and Clawley never touched the ball. Perhaps the Spurs did a little too much passing, but it was a treat to witness and stirred the pulses of some of the old 'uns who began to talk about Preston's palmy days. Only luck saved a score, and then United came with some ugly rushes.

Needham was grand and at times seemed to be playing the Spurs himself. The play got more even, and for a final tie it was a grand exhibition. Just when we all thought of the interval arriving without a score, United caught the Spurs' defence napping and Priest whizzed the ball past Clawley. This was hard lines on Spurs who had played better football and had much the best of the game.

The resumption saw a slight alteration in the play as the Spurs opened up the game. Beautiful work by the front rank left Cameron with the ball, and manipulating it superbly he beat Foulke with a lovely shot. And then the crowd let themselves go! They are sportsmen and recognized merit in these lads playing before a critical and hostile crowd. Hard knocks abounded and Needham with a lot of 'kid' got several verdicts that brought no result. What a raging game it was! Then Spurs got in one of those bewildering runs which has made them famous and Cameron shot, but the ball hit a United player and went out to Smith who, never hesitating, shot by Foulke with deadly accuracy. It was a proud moment for us all, as we realized we had won, but the hall mark had yet to come! The Sheffielders were in desperate straits, and corner after corner was conceded, and from one of these Johny Cameron tried his luck and dropped the ball right into goal, where Sandy Brown's famous head was waiting and Foulke was again beaten.

Every one of us went mad for a while, and the boys shook hands like squeaky pumps. We had won! Although Sheffield never gave up, the backs and Clawley were always there, and one of George's backhanders was a marvellous clearance. We all looked at our clocks, and slowly the minutes ticked off till Mr Kingscott sounded the retire and the famous game ended.

The Sheffield papers accepted the defeat generously. The *Sheffield Independent* observed: 'Spurs did with United what United have often done with others, and earned hearty congratulations by skill, pluck and keenness which showed that although the Cup has gone to a region which for long has not known it, it has fallen into worthy hands.' The *Sheffield Telegraph* added: 'United were manifestly outplayed, and it remains to be seen how far the fresh destination of the Cup will affect the game.'

It may be doubted if a Cup win has ever been celebrated in quite the way that Tottenham now relished theirs. Thousands of spectators rolled down onto the pitch to see Jack Jones receive the Cup from Lord Kinnaird, and thousands more lined the streets of Bolton as Tottenham's players moved in their brake towards the station . . . a journey broken by a halt at the Swan Hotel where the Cup was filled with champagne. The engine which took them back to London had a huge 'Tottenham' banner draped over its front and, behind, the celebrations began in earnest in two splendid Pullman diners.

Back in North London the streets were alive with people. The White Hart Hotel, at the entrance to the ground, was twinkling with fairy lights, the police station and even the fire stations at Coombes Croft and High Cross were decorated and illuminated, and private houses which did not dress themselves up were cold rarities. A roaring trade was done in horns, confetti, ostrich feathers and mourning cards for Sheffield United, and thousands of fans marched endlessly up and down bellowing out old tunes with new words in praise of their team.

The Spurs' special train was due to arrive at South Tottenham station at 12.35 a.m. on Sunday morning, and for two hours beforehand the road from Seven Sisters Corner was impassable. Trams ground to a halt as processions carrying Chinese lanterns pranced up and down outside the station. There were two bands there, one the Tottenham Town Band itself, and as the train puffed slowly in they struck up 'See the Conquering Hero Comes'. Rockets and other fireworks lit up the night sky and the cheers were probably heard back in Sheffield. The players had to force their way through the crush to their two brakes, Jones and the Cup leading the way, and once they were aboard the crowd unharnessed the horses and pulled their heroes all the way back to White Hart Lane. There were now about 30,000 people lining the roads and the journey back to the ground took an hour and a half. 'There were so many people, so tight together, you could have walked on their heads', said one report.

The celebrations began to wind down as the sun came up; but

Tottenham Hotspur Football Club, Limited.

HOTSPUR v SHEFFIELD CUP-TIE MATCHES.

ANIMATED PICTURES

Of the above Matches, shewing the play at the Crystal Palace and at Bolton,

WILL BE GIVEN ON THE

SPURS' FOOTBALL GROUND,

MONDAY EVENING, APRIL 29th.

Many other pictures of local interest will also be shewn by the Prestwich Manufacturing Company, of Tottenham.

TOTTENHAM BRASS BAND WILL BE IN ATTENDANCE.

ADMISSION, 6d. BOYS, 3d.

GATES OPEN 8 P.M. PICTURES 9 P.M.

IF the Spurs Win the Cup, a grand DISPLAY OF FIREWORKS

WILL CONCLUDE THE ENTERTAINMENT.

JOHN CAMERON, Secretary,
High-road, Tottenham.

An announcement in the local press advertising films of the two matches which took Spurs to the Cup.

they started again on Monday evening, when 12,000 people, bright-eyed and bent on business again, turned up at the ground to watch films – 'animated pictures' shown on a huge sheet in front of the stand – of the two matches. It proved to be more than just a night at the pictures. Under a bright moon there were more photographs (the centrepiece 'Bravo Spurs, you have won the Cup'), more singing, more music from the Tottenham Town Band and more dancing. The Cup stood in front of the stand while a replica was paraded around the ground.

The team, meanwhile, were obliged to play two Southern League games, at Luton and Kettering, on the Monday and Tuesday, and it says much for their stamina that they won the first and drew the second. Between the two games, for example, they had a night out in Luton where – according to the *Weekly Herald* – 'the manager was waiting at the Red Lion Hotel, a most commodious and comfortable hostelry, with a request that the team would honour "Woman and Wine". The Ladies were evidently desirous of smiling their appreciation of the merry Spurs. In this department the whole team scored heavily, but there was a general consensus of opinion that, as usual, the Bhoy from the Emerald Isle (Kirwan) was champion.'

As a writer in *Association Football and the Men Who Made It* (The Caxton Publishing Company, 1906) later declared: 'Than the famous Spurs there is probably no more popular club in England. Did they not recover the Association Cup for the south? Did they not play pretty and effective football? Are they not scrupulously fair? Are they not perfectly managed?' It was only a matter of time before they were welcomed into the League; and in 1908 they made it.

In just a quarter of a century they had moved from a High Road lamp-post, the second on the right towards Bruce Grove, to a place in football's high society.

3 Swindon... 1912

Swindon Town, a club of ruddy complexion and strong and honest rustic roots, have never played in the First Division of the Football League. It is a grave social injustice which the FA Cup has done much to temper.

Between Swindon's first Cup game in 1907 and the completion of the hundredth tournament in 1981 they beat First Division opposition on sixteen occasions. There is something deep within the soul of this Wiltshire club which obliges it to rebel against its natural place in football's society.

Swindon contributed an indelible line to the history of the game by winning a Wembley final when they were members of the Third Division; but that was in the League Cup, when they beat Arsenal by 3-1 in the 1969 final, and so belongs to another story. It was a triumph, nonetheless, which owed much to the club's noble traditions in the senior tournament.

Here is also a club which is a product of its environment, artisan but dignified, uncomplicated but designing, modest but progressive. Swindon is the county town of Wiltshire, seventy-seven miles west of London, and was once the home of the Great Western Railway Company, the best line in the world; a town, too, of agriculture, quarrying and clothing manufacture. The county itself is one of the least spoilt in the kingdom, a place of breezy space and rounded hills, its character unchanging and quite unmistakable.

It was here, in three seasons just before World War I, that Swindon Town put together a Southern League side that made nonsense of status and form in the Cup. They reached the semi-finals in 1910, the quarter-finals in 1911 and the semi-finals again in 1912. They were beaten in each of the semi-finals by the club which eventually won the trophy, Newcastle and then Barnsley, and in the second the issue was settled by a single goal scored in the second-half of a replay – and this after Swindon had missed a penalty. It was, by any yardstick, a remarkable achievement.

Swindon were at their peak in 1912, and as long as there were men who remembered them there were arguments that this was the best side the club ever produced. They began that season as Southern League champions and with a defeat that might have curdled the self-respect of a lesser team. They were beaten by 8 goals to 4 by Manchester United, the champions of the Football League, in the Charity Shield.

It was a defeat, however, for which the First Division was to pay. On their way to the semi-final Swindon beat two clubs from that exalted plane, Notts County in the second round and Everton, who were to finish the season as runners-up, in the quarter-finals. There was no room for argument about either victory: Swindon were the better team on the day.

Swindon now had a settled team of individual skill and collective directness, a team of character and muscular determination which was eager to test itself against members of the two divisions of the Football League at every opportunity. They were adaptable, consistent, good at improvising and relished the big occasion. They were ready for mighty deeds.

They also had one player, above all, who was fit to keep company with the best in the land. He was Harold John Fleming, an inside-forward of infinite variety and a man of many parts, cricketer, tennis-player, golfer, swimmer and, before football claimed him, a student at Warminster Theological College. He was brilliant, sensitive, unselfish and hugely admired, an artist with the ball, a weaver of patterns. He had a subtle swerve, a cannonball of a shot that was anything but subtle and an appetite for the game that made him one of the game's first 'roamers'. He moved about so effectively, sometimes quickly, sometimes stealthily but always with purpose, that he was almost impossible to pin down. Fleming was an England international who was a delight to watch but murder to play against. Even now small boys at the County Ground know of Fleming; and visitors who enter at the main door are reminded of him before every game. At the foot of the directors' stairs there is a handsome statue of the great man standing on a column.

Swindon, however, were in no sense a one-man team. Len

Skiller was a goalkeeper of rare authority, a man who dominated his area and had a sound understanding with his two full-backs, Harry Kay on the right, who was noted for his coolness and judgement, and John (Jock) Walker, a Scottish international, who was recognized as one of the finest left-backs of his time.

The Athletic News even broke into verse over Walker.

A light-haired son of Beith
Who southward came a-faring,
  A back of backs
  Who nothing lacks
Of courage and of daring;
  A credit to the land
Of brose and bowf and whiskey
  With but one fault
  He should cry 'Halt'
To methods somewhat risky

He holds opponents tight
  No-one could hold on tighter
  In splendid check
  Like Alan Breck
He is a 'bonnie fighter'
  And perhaps an English Cup
He may yet help to win; done
  It may be
  (We've yet to see)
By Walker's club – that's Swindon

Billy Tout at right-half was a thinking footballer, and the side's penalty expert, Frank Handley on the left, was fair-haired, hard and vigorous, while Billy Silto, in the middle, was a good-humoured man who learnt the game in a colliery village in his native Durham. 'Silto is energy personified,' observed one contemporary. 'He is an ideal intervener, adept at feeding his forwards and when the going is on the soft side he literally revels in the mud.'

The forward line, too, was an interesting mixture. Bob Jefferson, a right-winger with a notable Grecian nose, was capable of tight control at high speed; then came Fleming; Freddy Wheatcroft was a centre-forward who used his head intelligently both for putting the ball into the net and holding his line together; Archie Bown, at inside-left, was at his best inside the opposition penalty area, a player of quick reflexes and bullying tenacity; and Sammy Lamb on the wing had a lovely left foot that could place the ball to order on the run or from free-kicks and corners.

It was much too good a side to be extended at home by their opponents in the first round, a Nottinghamshire club called Sutton Junction, and Swindon won by five goals to nil. The *Sportsman* reported: 'Sutton were completely outclassed from beginning to end, play being so one-sided as to appear ridiculous. Particularly was this the case in the second-half when Swindon abandoned all attempts at forcing play giving themselves up to entertaining the crowd by an exhibition of juggling with the ball. Fleming alone seemed out for goal-getting.' Fleming was rewarded for his competitiveness with four goals, Bown scoring the other.

Notts County, in the second round, were a different proposition altogether. Here was a club of substance and tradition, members of the First Division, the oldest club in the Football League and winners of the Cup in 1894. Swindon were again at home and, despite a week of heavy frost, a combination of constant rolling, sand and brilliant sunshine on the day of the match left the pitch hard but not dangerous. The conditions suited the Wiltshire men admirably and 'The Pilot', writing in *The Athletic News*, was able to report: 'Swindon were a greatly superior side . . . on a frost bound pitch they hesitated not, but dashed in and many times caught their opponents napping by sheer dash and, some may say, recklessness.'

Swindon won by two goals to nil with the first, described here by the *Swindon Borough Press,* coming just before half-time: 'The ball went down to Lamb who centred to Fleming and the international wriggled right to the goal-line. West (County's left-back) sat down on the ball and gathered the ball between his legs and held it, but the Town's forwards swarmed over him. The excitement was intense, but finally when the ball was released the Town forwards literally ran it over the line, Jefferson being the man to obtain credit for the goal.'

Albert Ironmonger, County's goalkeeper, was the tallest

player in England (6ft 4ins and topped by a huge cap), with a character and sense of humour to match. He had a reach which seemed to stretch to order and was almost unbeatable on his day; but, more than that, he was noisy, temperamental, instantly likeable and hopelessly eccentric. Ironmonger's demanding voice could carry the length of the pitch to seek out and berate a referee; he would often move to a distant touch-line to take a throw-in; and he was even known to hold up a game by sitting on the ball in the middle of the field because something had upset him. There is also a story, one of football's favourites, that he once ran the full length of the pitch to take a penalty, smacked it against the crossbar, led the frantic charge back to the other penalty area and then, attempting to stop a shot, wildly sliced the ball into his own net. But it was Ironmonger who now kept County's hopes alive in their Cup-tie at the County Ground – and it wasn't until near the end that fine combination on the left by Bown and Lamb opened the way for Wheatcroft to score Swindon's second.

Swindon were drawn against another Southern League club, West Ham United, in the third round and this time they were away from home. There was no romance or charity in this game: it started promisingly but then developed into a bruising if thrilling confusion of heavy clashes and free-kicks which Swindon were hard pressed to draw with the help of a goal by Fleming. This was not Swindon's style, but in the replay four days later they got things right. They imposed their own style and tempo on their East London opponents and won with two 'own' goals from West Ham and two more, later in the game, from Jefferson and Wheatcroft.

It was time for Swindon's greatest test. They had moved through the first three rounds with brave conviction, scoring twelve goals and conceding only one, but in the quarter-finals they were now drawn to play Everton at the County Ground. Here was one of the founder members of the Football League, a club of huge resources and mighty repute who had been pressing hard for the championship almost every season since the turn of the century. They were again in the top three in the League, they were clear favourites to win the Cup and they had a forward line which cost (a figure, then, to raise eyebrows above the hairline) £5,000. Swindon's attack, by comparison, cost £75; Lamb was the only player for whom they had paid a fee.

Everton's goalkeeper was Billy Scott, an Irish international who was regarded by many as the best in Britain and whose younger brother, Elisha, was to become one of the legendary figures in Liverpool's history. Jock Maconnachie, at left-back, was a little man of wonderful strength who many years later was to join the Swindon staff. But it was at half-back and in their forward line that Everton's real strength lay. They were, above all, a side which loved to employ their skill and wit in attack.

Harry Makepeace, Everton's left-half, was one of the outstanding sporting figures of his time, an England international at both football and cricket and a man of the highest principles. He had been a member of Everton's Cup-winning side in 1906, a player of vision and variety but also a worker who, whatever the conditions, seemed quite indestructible. He made and scored goals with equal facility and could turn a game by himself. Oddly, though, he was a much less flamboyant cricketer. He was an opening batsman of great efficiency and patience who, as Neville Cardus once wrote, would sometimes accumulate runs with 'an odd air of sad distaste'. As a cricketer he prepared the way for others; as a footballer he wrote and played all the tunes.

In front Everton had an inside trio who could be devastatingly effective, three men who had been bought by Everton, generally believed to be the richest club in the country, because individually they were outstanding and together would pose problems beyond the solving of most defences. Frank Jefferis, the inside-right, was an England player with dazzling footwork whom Southampton had let go because they needed the money; Tom 'Boy' Browell had been levered away from Hull City, a nineteen-year-old centre-forward of so much promise that the Everton fans had come to expect at least one goal a game from him; and, at inside-left, there was Frank Bradshaw, once of Northampton and a man with a shot powerful enough to leave goalkeepers helpless on their line from thirty yards.

The mood in the pubs and clubs of Swindon was one of pessimism: a suspicion persisted that this time their team was facing more than it could handle. There was much else they could have talked about. News had just arrived that Captain Scott had reached the South Pole; Miss Pankhurst had gone to ground, but other suffragettes were going to prison, and there was a coal strike which had forced the local GWR sheds to lay off 7,000 men. But as the *Swindon Borough Press* reported: 'The sole topic of conversation among Swindonians since the draw was made has been whether Swindon are capable of beating the First Leaguers . . . There is no supporter, even the most partisan, but what realizes the gravity of the task.' Another writer in the *Borough Press* dismissed the pessimists curtly. 'Already there are those who think Swindon will meet their doom', he wrote. 'The writer is not included in this class of supporter and a win of 2-1 is predicted for Swindon.' Such omniscience!

On the eve of the match the *North Wilts Herald* took a broader look at the chemistry of the Cup:

> There is something ludicrous about these unequal contests the Cup competition possesses, a glamour and an attractiveness which are proof against apparent drawbacks, and while the amateur reformer is for ever cropping up with profound schemes which shall ensure absolute perfection there does not seem to be very much wrong with matters as they now stand. If a couple of teams are evenly matched so much the better; if a poor side is drawn against a strong one the weakling, except by a big fluke, goes to the wall, and that is its proper place.

Everton, for their part, were taking no chances. They trained on the bracing Lancashire coast during the week and travelled south on Friday, staying overnight at Oxford. They brought with them an army of supporters, and two hours before the kick-off, on 9 March 1912, most of them were already in place with straw hats, favours and umbrellas in blue and white. The eventual crowd, with Swindon drawing support from as far afield as Bristol, Devizes, Westbury, Trowbridge and Weymouth, totalled 13,989, with receipts (£933) just failing to reach £1,000 for the first time at the County Ground.

There was torrential rain in the morning and although the sun broke through brilliantly at lunch time there were still ominous-looking clouds on the horizon. The pitch itself carried a lot of surface water and local bandsmen had to move several times before they found a spot which didn't threaten them with pneumonia in the ankles. They also discovered they were expected to compete with hundreds of bells, horns and hooters — an unequal contest in which they soon conceded defeat.

Both teams were at full strength as Everton elected to kick towards the Stratton End, with a tricky wind now starting to blow directly across the ground. *Swindon:* Skiller, Kay, Walker; Tout, Silto, Handley; Jefferson, Fleming, Wheatcroft, Bown and Lamb. *Everton:* Scott; Stevenson, Maconnachie; Harris, Fleetwood, Makepeace; Beare, Jefferis, Browell, Bradshaw, Davidson. Referee: F. Heath (Birmingham).

Everton immediately showed they meant business. Makepeace was everywhere and a fierce drive by Browell grazed the topside of the Swindon bar. The First Division club obviously believed that the long, high ball was best suited to the conditions and for a while their methods looked like paying off. But Swindon began to work things out for themselves and the game became surprisingly fast, tightly balanced but of variable quality. Then, as the *Swindon Borough Press* reported, Swindon had a double break:

> Wheatcroft again obtained possession, and after shouldering Fleetwood off gave Jefferson a glorious opportunity which the right-winger took swift advantage of, for he shot hard and true right up under the bar.
>
> Then followed a scene of undescribable enthusiasm, which has seldom been equalled on the Swindon County Ground: caps and umbrellas and everything at hand being waved aloft. This lasted quite a minute. Everton wavered . . . and again Lamb was given possession and raced away to the other end where Stevenson was forced to give a corner. This was well placed and Bown headed the second goal for Swindon after 20 minutes play.

Swindon were two goals up before the game was quarter run! Up on the terraces there was now a buzz of incredulity. This, surely, was too good to be true. The County Ground waited for Everton's reply, and they did not have to wait long. The First Division side stepped up the pace of the game still further, with

Makepeace, above all, endlessly inventive; and early in the second half the England international got the bit of luck he now deserved. He lobbed the ball into the Swindon penalty area, it struck a defender's shoulder and Skiller – with loudly expressed disgust – watched it spin beyond his reach and into the net.

Everton, their combination now smooth and rhythmic, could have taken total control of the match at this point but Swindon, sensibly, kept calm and began to hit back with quick, powerful counter-attacks. The Everton storm started to fade and, as thousands of eyes watched the clock on the Press Box ticking away the seconds, it became apparent that the Southern League team were lasting better. Everton found enough steam to launch one last calculated onslaught – moments, these, of marvellous drama – but Swindon still looked in charge of the afternoon and when Mr Heath ended the game the pitch was immediately covered with the red and white of Swindon. The cheering and singing seemed to rattle the fabric of the stand. It was a moment no one wanted to let go.

The *Borough Press,* in a column engagingly called 'Swindon Chimes', summed up like this:

> It would be invidious to single out any of the Town players, for the whole team worked like a well oiled machine, every player extending every ounce of muscle . . . Silto marked Browell beautifully, Harold Fleming (despite an injured ankle) was still often brilliant, including a raid in the very last minute of the game which nearly produced another goal, Bown and Lamb made a dazzling left-wing pair, and Wheatcroft played one of the finest games of his career. Jefferson was in the right mood and Swindon's halves compared favourably with Everton's, while Kay and Walker were at least equal to the Everton pair. Skiller enhanced his reputation in goal still further.

There was a decorous postscript from 'Pilot' in *The Athletic News:*

> 'When Greek meets Greek, there comes the tug-of-war' was exemplified in the battle between Swindon and the mighty men of Everton . . . yet how dissimilar in method and actions. Everton were stylish all through, clever in con-

ception, neat in the working of mazy puzzles, gaining ground with machine-like combination. Swindon were meteoric in their Dervish-like rushes, apparently relying on the dourness of their defenders and the fleetness of their flying wingers. But there was brain and craft behind all these rushing forays. One resembled clever rapier work, while the other might be likened to the good, honest broadsword.

The pride of Swindon's townspeople in their football team was boundless. The *Swindon Evening Advertiser* proclaimed: 'In city and in town, in every village and remote hamlet where Soccer is followed, the victory must have occasioned intense delight, and even in the heart of the Metropolis cheered the hearts of many thousands.' The *North Wilts Herald,* not to be outdone, added: 'It was a game that will go down to posterity as being worthy to rank among the great games of a generation. It is left to Swindon – a little club with headquarters in a town of 50,000 inhabitants – to keep the Southern banner flying.'

The only note of discord was provided by the secretary of the Royal Society for the Protection of Birds who wrote thus to the *Swindon Advertiser:* 'It is to be hoped that the picture of two detestable young women wearing stuffed robins in their hats as a "compliment" to the Swindon football team is a libel and an invention. The footballers who call themselves by the name of our popular little red-breast can hardly be gratified by seeing the dead bodies of their mascot stuck on girls' heads; and if they possess the ordinary, healthy instinct of young Englishmen are more likely to hiss the wearers off the ground than to wish to walk out with them on Sunday" – (Miss) L. Sardiner.

The paper replied: 'This is really too funny for words . . . we must hasten to calm her feelings by at once assuring her that these "popular little red-breasts" are nothing more than felt, paper and wadding – in fact quite artificial! They can be bought in Swindon for one penny each.'

Swindon's opponents in the semi-finals were Barnsley of the Second Division – and a sharper contrast with the elegant men of Everton cannot be imagined. 'Battling Barnsley', they were called; and battlers they were – hard, rigidly disciplined, quite undentable and hugely patient. They were muscular stayers who had taken eight games to overcome Birmingham, Leicester

Fosse, Bolton and Bradford City, the Cup-holders, on their way to the semi-finals. Four of these games had been goalless draws (three against Bradford in a tie which took nearly seven hours to settle) and, in all, they had conceded only four goals.

A crowd of 48,057 went to Stamford Bridge for the semi-final, and doubtless left wondering if their journey had been worthwhile. It was another goalless draw – Barnsley's fifth of their Cup run – and a game almost devoid of merit. Barnsley laid into Swindon like foxes in a chicken run and Fleming, whose skill was the most obvious threat to them, received special attention. He had to leave the field before half-time and, although he returned, he was little more than a passenger. He was dazed and clearly in pain and fifteen minutes before the end he limped out of the game with, among other things, a nasty groin injury. Fleming did not play again for ten months.

Barnsley made no new friends that day. The Swindon supporters kept up an incessant cry of 'Dirty Barnsley' to which the Barnsley fans, happy witnesses to the slaughter, replied: 'Poor Cock Robin'. Then the papers had their say. 'It was apparent that Harold Fleming was to be a "marked man" in every sense of the word', said the *Morning Leader*. 'No sooner did this dangerous forward get hold of the ball within shooting distance than his legs seemed to be mysteriously shot out from under him. Barnsley were out to stop Fleming at all costs.'

The *People* declared: 'The Swindon and International inside-right was treated even worse than he usually is, and the battering culminated in his being compelled to leave the field in the closing stages with a leg that had no power to do its accustomed work and, I imagine, ribs so cruelly tender that a further upset would have put him in hospital.' The *Daily Express* was even more to the point: 'Barnsley's treatment of one of the cleanest players who ever donned a football boot was – not to put too fine a point upon it – disgraceful. To stop a clever opponent by maiming him is not football as understood in the south. It is certainly not "cricket".'

Swindon were without Fleming and Tout for the replay at Meadow Lane, the home of Notts County, on the following Wednesday, another tight dour game which always seemed likely to be settled by a single goal. Swindon's chance came when Jefferson was bowled over and they were awarded a penalty. Tout would normally have taken it and scored: he was an expert at the job. But who would take the responsibility now? Swindon had not given the problem a thought! No one volunteered and, after some discussion, Bown reluctantly agreed to have a go. He hit the ball cleanly enough but Cooper, the Barnsley goalkeeper, made a wonderfully athletic save . . . a save that proved to be the key to the final.

Ten minutes into the second half Skiller was forced to concede a corner, Bartrop, the Barnsley right-winger, took it and Bratley, their tall centre-half who had moved up for the kick, headed the ball firmly into a corner of the net. Barnsley kept a clamp-like grip on their lead and, in the end, they were worth their win. In the end, too, they were worthy Cup winners. They met West Bromwich Albion in the final at the Crystal Palace and, for the sixth time, they were involved in a goalless draw. The replay was at Bramall Lane, Sheffield, and after ninety minutes there was still no score; and only two minutes of extra time were left when someone, somewhere, decided that enough was enough. Harry Tuffnell, the Barnsley inside-right, dribbled artfully through the Albion defence before scoring with a sweetly struck ground shot – it was the sort of goal which ought to settle every Cup Final.

Swindon, meanwhile, were on their way to South America for a tour of Argentina, Brazil and Uruguay. It was all part of the club's growing-up process and, under their genial manager Sam Allen, who was involved with the club in one capacity or another for fifty years, they won six and drew two of their eight matches. It rounded off a season of high success, a season more arduous than any other in their young history, a season in which they had woven themselves into the pride and traditions of their Wiltshire community. There could be no going back, and eight years and a world war later they became one of the original members of the Third Division of the Football League.

4 Charlton... 1923

Charlton Athletic's success in their first season in the Cup as a League club was a piece of gross but sublime impertinence. As members of the newly formed Third Division South, they beat three First Division clubs, all former winners of the Cup, in a way which suggested they could even win the trophy themselves – and this in 1923, the year of the first final at Wembley.

Charlton overcame Manchester City away from home and then Preston North End and West Bromwich Albion at the Valley, before going down by a single goal to Bolton; and Bolton, in turn went on to beat West Ham United in a final played before the King of England and a crowd of 200,000 which had squeezed into a stadium built to accommodate little more than half that number.

Perhaps the all-knowing Divinity who arranges these matters had originally intended Charlton to reach the final. Perhaps, then, he changed his mind. After all there was to be drama enough at Wembley's first football match; the unscheduled presence there of one of the game's little adventurers, another club from the melting-pot of East London, might have been inviting trouble with which even police-constable George Scorey and his white horse could not have coped.

In any case, Charlton's success introduced them to the wider stage of the game in the most effective and spectacular way possible. The season before, their first in the League, they had finished an anonymous sixteenth in the Third Division South; but now, little more than one year on, they were one of the most talked-about teams in the land. They were attracting bold headlines – "Miracle-working Babes rout Lancastrians", "Charlton Make History" and "Onward the Reds, ever onward". They even enriched the knowledge of working-class England. From saloon-bars in the north to pier-ends in the south, people were suddenly aware that the district of Charlton was a remarkably unremarkable corner of old Woolwich, just south of the point where the Thames straightens out through the busiest part of London's dockland and heads for the sea.

Some intrepid souls had even followed their team there; they knew the ground itself, the Valley, a giant bowl of an arena close to the main road and railway. It was impressive in a spartan sense. Part of the vast eastern terrace, for example, was little more than a chalk cliff offering a superb view in exchange for nothing more than a gamble with life or limb. There was a stand, dressing-rooms and some proper terracing, but the Valley was not a place of any obvious charm. What most people did not realize, however, was that Charlton were living on a high-octane mixture of ambition and fear. It made their Cup run in 1923 all the more remarkable.

Charlton was a young club, with its roots in the streets, local parks and mission halls of the parish, but it was not properly packaged and launched until 1905, when it entered the Lewisham League (Division Three). By the start of the first World War, the club had progressed to senior football in the Southern Suburban League and played on four different grounds, Sieman's Meadow (which became a rubbish dump), Woolwich Common (to which they had to carry the goalposts a full mile), Pound Park (with their headquarters in a local pub) and Horn Lane (on the edge of Greenwich marshes).

Horn Lane became a petrol store during the war and, obliged to find yet another ground before they could resume playing, the club discovered the Valley, the hillside bowl that was to become their permanent home. They played their first game there in 1919 and Jimmy Seed, later to become Charlton's secretary-manager for twenty-three years, was to recall his first game there as a Tottenham player.

'What a dump it was in those days,' he remembered. 'I could hardly believe how dreary it was when I played there for Spurs' reserves in a friendly game in 1920. It was wet, cold and miserable but there were no bath or showers for us afterwards and we even had to walk to a nearby hut to change back into dry clothes. There was no stand, either, and players had to eat in a local pub – and that was where they earned their terrible nickname of "*The Addicks*". The pub served them with boiled haddock, a fact which local Cockneys soon latched onto.

Charlton, though, were now a club in a hurry. They turned professional in 1920, joined the Southern League for the 1920-21 season and the following year were elected to the Third Division (Southern section) of the Football League, which was just a year old. It says much for the club's players that despite their lack of material comforts they were achieving enough on the pitch to make this rapid promotion possible.

The club's directors decided the omens were right for heavy investment. They were in a heavily populated area which seemed to enjoy its football, they had no major competition locally and in 1921, in anticipation of big crowds, they committed themselves to spend the then enormous sum of £14,000 on a grandstand, dressing rooms and terracing. There were immediate snags. The contractors fell beind schedule – the new facilities were not ready until late the following year – and gates fell so far below expectations that for most of 1922 they were losing £100 a week. They needed help; and it came, providentially, in the shape of their mighty Cup run.

Charlton had not competed in the Cup the previous season because their election to Division Three was confirmed only after the tournament's exemptions were settled. Their side, then, came fresh to the challenge, a side which was to be unchanged throughout the major part of their Cup run. It was a side, too, which contained eight players born in the London area and a side which had cost only £300 to put together – that was the fee paid to Chelsea for their inside-left Bob Thomson.

The team was rich in character. Freddy Wood was an athletic goalkeeper with quick reflexes and sound judgement who had played for Crystal Palace and Millwall before joining Charlton in the summer of 1922. The full-backs, Frank Burton and Baden Herod, were a strong, disciplined pair. Burton, 6ft 1½ins and 12½ stone, was born in Mexico and known as 'Bronco', a formidable defender who had previously been with Queen's Park Rangers and West Ham. He also had a distinguished war record, being wounded six times, and among his many decorations was the Croix de Guerre. Few opponents relished an afternoon in his company. Herod's full name, splendidly, was Edwin Redvers Baden Herod, a loyal and popular man from Ilford who clearly enjoyed his football. He was quick of mind and movement, and his clearances always had a purpose.

Albert Purdy, Charlton's right-half, was an alert and busy player from Edmonton who was later to become Fulham's groundsman and, in fact, to live in the famous cottage at Craven Cottage for more than thirty years. Seth Plum, at left-half, was a former Royal Navy man, a richly talented amateur who before the season was out was to help England's full international side beat France by four goals to one in Paris; it was, oddly, his only cap.

The central pillar of the side was Arthur Whalley, who was not only their captain and centre-half but guide, friend and counsellor to everyone at the club. He had learnt his trade with Manchester United, first as an understudy to the great Charlie Roberts and then as a first-team player in his own right on nearly a hundred occasions between 1912 and 1920. Whalley then moved, briefly, to Southend, before joining Charlton in 1921, a straight, powerful man who led by doughty example and carefully chosen word. There were times during Charlton's Cup run when his contribution was nothing less than heroic. His experience was invaluable, his enthusiasm immeasurable. Whalley was a man who cared about his club.

Syd Castle, Charlton's outside-right, had come from Basingstoke, a twenty-eight-year-old with a broad, dimpled grin and a rare turn of pace, an elusive player who could make opposing defenders feel tearful and who combined well with Alex Steele at inside-right. Steele was a Belfast man, already an amateur international and later to win four full caps for Ireland. His strength was inside the penalty area, but although he was Charlton's leading marksman in the League he did not score once in their Cup run.

Albert Abraham Goodman (known affectionately as 'Kosher') was Charlton's centre-forward and the big surprise of the season. In the first half of the season he had played at right-back, left-back, centre-half, left-half and inside-left, but was switched to centre-forward for the first-round game against Manchester City. He scored a goal, kept his place and then also scored against both Preston and West Bromwich. His value before the switch had been useful but rarely outstanding – he had played sixteen games for Tottenham in their Second Division promotion season in 1919-20. But as a centre-forward he proved himself quite unlike any other in the League, unorthodox, unpredictable, perplexing. His contribution to Charlton's Cup run rivalled even that of Whalley.

Bob Thomson, the one man in the side to cost a transfer fee, also played his full part, an inside-left who knew his own strengths and limitations as well as he knew the game. He was a man with a mind of his own (and a distinguishing quiff of hair), who had played for Chelsea in the war-time Cup Final of 1915. He scored a couple of goals in the Cup run and brought the best out of Steve Smith, his left-winger, who was the son of the Aston Villa and England player of the same name. Smith was lively, quick-witted and able to centre accurately on the run.

Charlton met two other Third Division clubs at the Valley in the fifth and sixth qualifying rounds. They beat Northampton (fellow members of the Southern section) by 2-0 and then Darlington (Northern) by 2-1, with Darlington missing a penalty only a few minutes from the end. They were worthy victories, but nobody saw them as a team likely to uproot any trees in the Cup. They had had home advantage in both games and, firmly positioned in mid-table, they had no realistic hopes of promotion. Thus, when they were drawn to play Manchester City at Hyde Road in the first round proper it was widely and reasonably assumed that all Charlton would get out of the tie was a pleasant day's outing.

Manchester City were a First Division club of eminence, who had won the Cup in 1904 and finished runners-up to Burnley in the championship of 1920-21. It was also a club about to play its last Cup game at Hyde Road, with its confined space and labyrinth of corridors. A major fire had gutted the main stand, the lease of the ground was running out and they were soon to move to their present ground, Maine Road, on Moss Side.

The City side had been put together with imagination. J.F. Mitchell was an amateur goalkeeper who had been signed from Preston and played in horn-rimmed spectacles kept in place by a band round his head; a goalkeeper, for all that, of the highest quality. Sammy Sharp, at right-half, was renowned for his fiercesome sliding tackles, and Charlie Pringle, who married the legendary Billy Meredith's daughter, was a left-half full of character and craft. T.C.F. Johnson, at centre-forward, was another amateur, a dashing opportunist who was later to play for England at full international level, and Horace Barnes, the inside-left, was reputed to be the hardest striker of a dead ball in football.

Hyde Road gave Charlton a generous hand as they took the field. The London side were cast in the role of sacrificial lambs and as they lined up the crowd of nearly 29,000 relaxed good-humouredly. The teams: *Manchester City* – Mitchell; Cookson, Wilson; Sharp, Hamill, Pringle; Kelly, Roberts, Johnson, Barnes, Murphy. *Charlton* – Wood; Burton, Herod; Purdy, Whalley, Plum; Castle, Steele, Goodman, Thomson and Smith.

The feeling of complacency soon gave way to mild concern, however, as Charlton's defence comfortably resisted the best City could throw at them; indeed, nearly forty minutes had gone before Wood in the London club's goal was forced to save a worthwhile shot – and this despite the fact that Whalley had opened up a cut he received at Watford the week before and had to leave the field for a few minutes to have his head heavily bandaged.

Three minutes before half-time City's growing doubts were justified when Smith cleverly eluded Sammy Cookson on Charlton's left, centred perfectly and Goodman headed past Mitchell. City decided to change their tactics during the interval and early in the second half, with the tempo of their game notably sharper, a centre by Murphy gave Johnson the chance to equalize. But now Whalley took control of the match, despite his bandaged head, and, according to the *Kentish Independent,* he 'presented a heroic figure, his fine generalship and ripe judgement of incalculable service to his side'.

It was a masterly performance that was to be rounded off in story-book fashion. Seven minutes from the end Mickey Hamill, City's Irish international centre-half, was hurried into making a mistake that led to a corner. Castle floated it across accurately and Whalley's bandaged head forced the ball home. The final score: Manchester City 1, Charlton 2 – and the *Kentish Independent* summed up: 'The Reds saw their chance to win and they took it with both hands, so to speak. They hustled the City defence and under pressure the home halves and backs became somewhat disorganized. The "Babes" stayed the pace better than their more distinguished opponents – and made history.' The City flag was immediately lowered to half-mast and Charlton returned to London to find a big, happy crowd waiting to welcome them at Euston.

There was to be no respite for Charlton. In the second round they were drawn at home to Preston who had won the League and Cup in 1889 without losing a match, and who in 1922 had been beaten by Huddersfield in the last of three finals to be played at Stamford Bridge and the first final to be decided by a penalty. There was a familiar name in the Preston goal that day – J.F. Mitchell. Within weeks of being beaten by that Huddersfield penalty he was transferred to Manchester City.

Preston were the first Division One side to play at the Valley and a side which had cost £15,000 to put together – approximately the sum Charlton had invested in making their ground fit for League football and which was now giving them daily heartburn. They were a team of less finesse but more muscle than in the days of the 'Invincibles', with Joe McCall at centre-half, the strong, experienced former England captain, the man who held them together. Only one of their side, however, was familiar to Charlton, Irish international James Ferris, who had previously played for Chelsea. He was best known as an inside-forward but was switched to outside-left for the game at the Valley. Charlton were unchanged and the Preston team was Branston; Hamilton, Doolan; Laird, McCall, Crawford; Rawlings, Jefferis, Roberts, Woodhouse, Ferris.

Preston began impressively and for ten minutes the difference between First and Third Division football seemed enormous. The Lancashire side were machine-like in their accuracy and Charlton, with grit and some luck, just hung on. Slowly, though, the balance of the game changed, Purdy and Plum began to have an influence in midfield and Goodman, Steele and Castle all missed chances.

The first half was goalless and at this point the *Kentish Mercury* takes up the story:

On resuming one anticipated that Preston would bring the

'shock tactics' they are noted for into play, but the boot was on the other foot, for within two minutes they found themselves a goal down. Roberts, their centre-forward, was pulled up for off-side and Burton, taking the kick, placed the ball up to Goodman who scored a grand goal with a first time drive from 20 yards out, the visitors' goalie probably never seeing it until he picked it out of the net. As was to be expected, this rattled the men from Preston and they went all out for an equalizer, but they failed to make an impression upon a defence that were playing a fine, resolute game.

Fourteen minutes later Steele received a pass from Whalley and he in turn transferred to Smith who, taking the ball in his stride, crashed in a fine shot which, striking the underneath of the cross-bar, gave Branston 'no earthly'. Preston re-arranged their attack and made desperate efforts to reduce the deficit, and it was during one of these bursts that Herod was adjudged guilty of pushing in the penalty area. Rawlings, the outside-right, was entrusted with the kick, but sent the ball yards wide of its intended destination. It must be admitted that till the end the visitors never gave up trying, and their outstanding player was McCall, their veteran centre-half, who, time without number, came to their rescue, but nothing they did put the 'Reds' goal in jeopardy, who to sum it up briefly, won and won well.

Charlton's supporters relished the moment. Many had hardly believed their side's first-round victory in Manchester, but now they had seen for themselves and, as the last whistle sounded, thousands clambered over the fences and attempted to catch the players before they left the field. Only Castle was trapped and, like a cork on a high sea, he was shouldered around in triumph. The crowd then gathered in front of the stand and demanded an appearance from the other players. Goodman appeared briefly, waved modestly and said a few words that were lost in the hullabaloo. McCall, Preston's hero, came out next and his message came over loud and clear. 'Your team surprised ours today', he said, 'and I hope you'll win the Cup.' The call for Charlton's players continued and at last Whalley himself appeared; and he did not waste his chance. The team, he said, would continue 'to give good, clean football' but in return the public would have to support them in still greater numbers. The faithful cheered again and then happily went home to tea. Charlton, in fact, had never been watched by a bigger crowd – 22,490 people paying £1,402 for the privilege of being there – and there were even better things to come.

Forty-eight hours later the draw for the third round gave Charlton another home tie against First Division opposition, West Bromwich Albion, and applications for tickets, especially for the 2,400 stand seats at 5s 9d a time, rolled in from all over London and Kent. Charlton decided to make extra terracing available on Cliff Side, they improved the banking in other areas and there was even optimistic talk of a crowd of more than 50,000.

Albion had many household names in their side and were hugely attractive opposition. Hubert Pearson was a splendidly built goalkeeper and renowned for his long kicks, Joe Smith, at right-back, was an England international and so, too, was Tommy Magee, a 5ft 3in right-half who was known as the 'Mighty Atom' and who had signed for Albion whilst in the trenches in France. Sid Bowser was a quick and accomplished player who made his name as a goal-scoring inside-forward but later switched to centre-half, and Bobby McNeal at left-half had been a miner in the north-east and signed forms for Albion on a billiard table in a local working men's club. Ivor Jones, their inside-left, was a brilliant ball-player, Stan Davies was a centre-forward famed for his dribbling and thunderous shooting, and Freddy Morris and Harry Gregory formed a left-wing partnership which could be devastating.

Smith, Magee, Bowser, McNeal and Morris were all England internationals and Jones and Davies had played for Wales. It was also a side cemented by loyalty: Smith played for Albion for sixteen years, missing only five games out of 250 between 1919 and 1925, and Magee, Bowser and McNeal each played more than 400 games for Albion. Pearson was the father of Harold Pearson, also a goalkeeper, who was to play for Albion and England, and Ivor Jones, a member of the famous Jones family of Swansea, was to be the father of Cliff Jones of Wales and a member of the celebrated Tottenham side which completed the League and Cup double in 1960-61.

The Valley, on that last Saturday of February in 1923, seemed to be the most popular place in London. Roads near the ground were choked with people and vehicles a couple of hours before the kick-off, long crocodiles of fans led to every turnstile, marshals with megaphones did their best to maintain some sort of order and pick-pockets had a field day, though some were caught and one old offender was later given six months' hard labour. The crowd, eventually, totalled 31,480 and when Whalley led his team out he remarked that the cheer which met them 'must be heard down in Brighton'. Charlton were unchanged once more and the West Bromwich line-up was Pearson; Smith, Adams; Magee, Bowser, McNeal; Spencer, Jones, Davies, Morris and Gregory.

Whalley won the toss but Albion were soon playing with style and confidence. Charlton seemed content to defend, but perhaps they had little choice at this stage because their own wingers were being tightly marked and Magee and McNeal, the Albion wing-halves, were on top of their game, reading the match intelligently, intercepting well and providing their forwards with a stream of incisive passes. But Charlton slowly began to get the hang of things, with Whalley again their key figure. Smoothly, almost unobtrusively, he began to push the ball through to Thomson and Steele, then Castle and Smith started to find more room on the wings and the whole balance of the game changed.

Charlton were now holding their own, their belief in themselves seemed total and early in the second half the Third Division club scored what was to prove the only goal of the match. The *Kentish Independent* described it in endearing detail: 'Goodman swung the ball out to Plum who feinted to pass but instead of doing so he beat his opponent and sent across a smart centre. Thomson swung round and shot at goal, but the ball struck an opposing back (who had dropped back into goal) and then cannoned off this defender to Pearson who was so surprised that he failed to get the leather, and Goodman rushed in and banged the ball into the net.'

Albion tried everything they knew, a fine side playing for their pride, but the army of Charlton fans up on the mountain slopes of the Valley seemed to sense long before the end that the day belonged to them; and, once again, when the final whistle went they clambered joyfully over the fences and ran to the front of the grandstand. This time Whalley refused to come out, but Freddy Wood did – 'It's because I'm the goalkeeper', he shouted. 'I'm the only one left with enough 'wind' to speak.'

'The scenes of enthusiasm at the end', reported the *Kentish Mercury*, 'were a fitting climax to a game well fought out in a style typical of the best traditions of English Cup football, and won by a team which, if not so clever individually as their opponents, were more effective collectively, and played with that perfect understanding which indicates tremendous possibilities and may well carry them on their way to figure in the grand finale at Wembley at the first time of asking.'

It was a partial opinion happily endorsed by a *London Evening News* reporter: 'I would not write Charlton Athletic down as a great team, but rather as a team of great-hearted triers, and in Cup football as we know it today that is almost everything. From a purely academic point of view, the Albion, even in the hour of defeat, played more scientific football, but the little Kentish club thoroughly deserved to win. If asked to explain in a few words the amazing success of this comparatively obscure Third Division club I should say it was their "will to win".'

Charlton's corner of London was now convinced that nothing was beyond them, and they remained so even when the draw for the quarter-finals paired them with First Division opposition for the fourth tie in succession. This time it was to be Bolton Wanderers, who had finished sixth in the championship in 1920, third the next year and sixth again in 1922. Their attack was formidable, with David Jack at inside-right, a tall and graceful predator, and Joe Smith and Ted Vizard forming the most lethal left-wing in football. Joe Smith of England had scored thirty-eight League goals in the 1920-21 season, which is still a club record, while Vizard of Wales was a wickedly elusive dribbler. There were eight internationals in the Bolton side and once again Charlton seemed to be hopelessly out of their class. The papers all tipped Bolton to win but this time there was a difference: most allowed themselves the luxury of a little safety clause. 'Charlton', wrote one, 'cannot wholly be trusted to remember their station in life.'

The *Kentish Independent's* view of Charlton's Cup run in 1923

The gates opened at midday, three hours before the kick-off, because Charlton could only guess at the size of the crowd the game might attract. It immediately proved a wise decision because by one o'clock on that March day in 1923 there were already 20,000 inside the ground, and supporters were being asked to help the marshals with their packing. Cheap railway tickets brought fans to the Valley from all points of the compass, trams and buses were full and, inside the stadium, club officials commended themselves on their foresight in erecting extra crush-barriers.

Charlton were again unchanged and they had never been in better shape. They had prepared for the game at Freshwater on the Isle of Wight as guests of the club chairman, Councillor D.W. Oliver, and they looked relaxed but determined as they took the field. But Bolton, too, looked as if they meant business. Their team was; Pym; Rowley, Finney; Nuttall, Seddon, Jennings; Butler, Jack, John Smith, Joe Smith and Vizard. The crowd, 42,033, was easily the biggest the Valley had housed, with receipts amounting to nearly £2,800.

This time, however, there was to be a change in the script. Charlton held their own throughout a hard and even game but the only goal of the afternoon was scored by Bolton; and it was the celebrated combination of Vizard, Joe Smith and Jack which produced it ten minutes before half-time. Vizard began the movement with neat control and a quick start near the halfway line. He exchanged passes twice with Joe Smith, a superb link-up which drew the Charlton defence irresistibly towards them, and when the ball was clipped inside it found Jack unmarked and about twelve yards from goal. Poor Freddy Wood did not even get near the shot. It was enough to win a game of furious movement but few chances.

Charlton were out of the Cup, after a run which had captured the imagination of the whole country; but they were lucky that all their success was not overshadowed by tragedy. Twice railings at the Station End were broken, once just before the start and again – more seriously – early in the game when spectators on the upper terraces pushed forward and then over balanced. There was a snowball effect until the pressure in front was so great that fences collapsed and a tide of humanity spilt onto the pitch. There were no major injuries but one young fan was carried away in the arms of Charlton's manager Walter Rayner. Order was quickly restored, though, and play continued while the breaches were repaired with stakes and scaffold poles.

The crisis seemed over but, alas, there was worse to come. Shortly before half-time the railings gave way again, men, women and children were thrown forward even more violently, finishing in a struggling heap, and the referee immediately stopped the game. Players were among the first rescuers and they were joined in seconds by a large possee of policemen and ambulance workers who had been watching nervously since the early trouble. Many of the fans at the bottom of the pile were small boys and girls who had been allowed to stand at the front to get a better view, and several were unconscious by the time they were reached. One little girl, carried by a policeman, was crying for her mother who was lying motionless in the arms of an ambulance man.

Minor hurts were treated on the field but about two dozen spectators were taken to the club's recreation room which was converted into a temporary ward. The more seriously hurt were then transferred to Greenwich Hospital, though, happily, all were to be released within a day or two. It could have been a tragedy of the worst kind and, properly, there were meetings at which pointed questions were asked. The wonder was that no one was maimed or killed – and that the game was allowed to continue. It says much for the composure of the players that they were still able to put together a memorable Cup-tie which was honorably won and bravely lost.

It was to be Bolton's year. They beat Sheffield United 1-0 in the semi-final at Old Trafford and then, fully conscious of their role in history, they overcame West Ham 2-0 in Wembley's first and most memorable final. More than 200,000 people (official attendance 126,047) saw David Jack, who was soon to play for England and later to join Arsenal for the first £10,000 transfer fee, score the first goal of all in the new home of English football. It was the start of the most successful period in Bolton's history. They won the Cup again in 1926 and 1929.

Meanwhile, poor Charlton floundered. Their supporters

proved stonily ungrateful for the excitement of the Cup run. Gates fell sharply and money problems increased to such an extent that later in the very same year Charlton's directors decided to make a new start on a ground at Catford. It was a disastrous decision, doomed by rising costs, delay and even smaller crowds, and within twelve months the club returned to the Valley.

Charlton's Cup run had given them a taste of success for the first time, but more than another decade was to pass before they again interested the nation as a whole. In two seasons between 1934 and 1936 they climbed from Third to First Division and, bridging the Second World War, they held onto that status for fourteen years. They also reached the first two Cup Finals after the war, losing the first to Derby in extra time but then beating Burnley with a late goal – again in extra time – by Chris Duffy.

Now, sadly, there is a generation which knows Charlton only as a club devoted to bouncing gently between the Second and Third Divisions. Somewhere inside the slopes of the Valley there is something much better waiting its turn.

5 Walsall...1933

The story of arguably the most celebrated giant-killing act of all is nicely illustrated by a bust and a ball. The bust is in bronze and stands on a pedestal of marble just inside the noble entrance hall of Arsenal Stadium. The football is made of leather in the old-fashioned way, broad-panelled and mud-coloured, and sits in a glass case in the secretary's office of Walsall's home at Fellows Park.

There is the merest of smiles on the face of the bust and boldly cut into the pedestal is a name and a legend – 'Herbert Chapman'. He was the first and possibly the greatest of all the great managers, a man who twice built a side that was good enough to win the League championship in three successive seasons – with Huddersfield in the 1920s and Arsenal in the 1930s. Chapman's Arsenal, above all, stood alone; they were invincible, grandly untouchable, a team of international repute in a parochial world. They were loved by their own but cordially hated by just about everyone else. The English game had a Highbury complex.

The ball represents the high-water mark in Walsall's history, indeed their only true peak, for here is a club which has never played First Division football and never reached even the quarter-finals of the Cup. They are among the foot-soldiers of the game, stubbornly unglamorous but an essential part of the structure.

Early in 1933, however, the third round of the Cup brought together Walsall, who were then marking time in the northern section of the Third Division, and Arsenal, who were in the process of winning the first of their three successive championships. A victory for Chapman and his team was regarded as a fact before the game began, as certain as Monday following Sunday, as predictable as the sun rising in the east. It was a moment for which the Cup, our old deceiver, had been waiting a long time. Twice Walsall's precious ball was put into the Arsenal net . . . and now, on that same stud-scarred ball there is a little silver medallion, surrounded by laurel leaves, which says simply: 'F.A. Cup 3rd round, January 14th 1933, Walsall 2 Arsenal 0.'

It is said that the voices of BBC news-readers trembled with surprise when they read out the result that evening. The *Birmingham Post* reported: 'It was a triumph so utterly bewildering that hours later one heard ordinarily level-headed businessmen demanding of their neighbours whether the thing they had seen with their own eyes had really happened, and being assured that their dilapidated headgear was incontrovertible evidence that they had not been dreaming.' Russell Stannard, a *Sunday Express* reporter, added: 'I formally resign the job of football prophet. Last week I said positively in large black capital letters that Arsenal would NOT lose at Walsall. So did sundry other football prophets. We were all wrong, and we all think it would be grand to be bloomin' well dead.'

Walsall immediately became a town of two quite separate factions: those who had seen the match and those who hadn't. A place at Fellows Park on that famous day and the right to say 'I was there' conferred new status in the community. This was instant history and now, half a century later, the constant retelling and repolishing of the story has given it a lovely patina.

Walsall's victory, moreover, had more than sporting significance. It was socially important at a time when the country was miserably crippled by recession and unemployment. The Black Country was largely on the dole, depression hung over the area like thick cloud and the football grounds stood almost alone as rallying points for local pride. They gave men purpose and dignity for the price of a couple of square feet on the terraces.

Walsall even launched its own brave little campaign to ginger up the local economy. It was called a 'Spending for Employment' campaign and, by way of notice and newspaper advertisement, the townspeople were urged to spend as much as they could afford and thus provide more work in the area. 'It may be that you can only afford to have your boots repaired', read the notices, 'or it may be that you can afford to build yourself a new home or at least have yours properly repaired or painted or your garden dug over. Or may be you can afford a new dress or suit. It does not matter which so long as you keep in view the prospect of giving some extra employment by putting your money into circulation. Spending provides employment – so spend now.'

It could hardly be claimed that even in better times Walsall had much going for it. A popular World Gazetteer of the time devoted 21 lines, for example, to the Russian city of Nijni-Novgorod, 17 lines to the Mexican frontier state of Coahuila, and 13 lines to the Devonshire market town of Tavistock whose population at the time was just over 4,000. Walsall was summarily dismissed in six lines: 'County borough and market town of Staffordshire. It is 8m N.W. of Birmingham and is served by the L.M.S. Railway and by canals. The principal trade is saddlery and hardware. Walsall sends one member to Parliament. Market days, Tues. and Sat. Pop. 103,102.'

The local Chamber of Commerce, to do its members justice, was aware that their town was never likely to be a honeypot for tourists. But they had their pride: one meeting got thoroughly upset because they were constantly receiving letters addressed to 'Walsall, near Birmingham' – a member claimed it should be 'Birmingham, near Walsall.' It was decided that Walsall needed promoting. The town, they agreed, should be 'further advertised'. They did not know that within a matter of days their local football team was to turn the name of Walsall into a household word.

The history of the town's football club, in keeping with everything else, had been stunningly ordinary. They became founder-members of Division Two of the Football League in 1892 and immediately gained one of their few imperishable distinctions – they were the first club to finish bottom of the new section. They failed to gain re-election three years later, returned to the League in 1896, lost their place again in 1901 and did not get back this time until twenty years later when the membership of the Third Division was doubled and split into northern and southern sections. Walsall were still below stairs, still trying, still hoping, when the Cup beckoned in 1933. It was a deserving choice.

Walsall were fifty-four places below Arsenal in the League, tenth in the northern section of Division Three with twenty-four points from twenty-four games. They were unbeaten at home but had not won away. The week before the Arsenal game they drew 1-1 at home to Barnsley; the week after they lost 2-0 at Hartlepools. The raw clay was not too promising.

Their team was a standard Third Division mixture of men on the way up or on the way down, or men who had never even taken off. Joe Cunningham, their goalkeeper, was 6ft 1in and a Scot who had reached Walsall by way of Aberdeen, Newport and Queen's Park Rangers. Jack Bennett, at right-back, was a Nottinghamshire man who had played for Birmingham and Blackpool, a long kicker, a strong tackler; and Sid Bird – 'Sid the Silent' – was a north-easterner who had come from Fulham, a broad and muscular left-back who did his job with no fuss and much efficiency.

Johnny Reed, the right-half, was another north-easterner, a former Wolves player, who had started his career as an inside-forward, while Harry Salt, on the left, was a Sheffielder who had been troubled by injuries. Salt had joined Walsall from Brentford, a player noted more for his energy than his finesse and a player who was eager to re-establish his place in the first team. George Leslie was a young centre-half who had looked distinctly raw when he joined Walsall from Charlton, but who had developed quickly into a formidable defender. He stood over six foot, weighed a solid thirteen stone and was essentially a stopper.

The forward line contained a bit of everything. Billy Coward, the right-winger, was the smallest and trickiest player in the side. He had previously played for Queen's Park Rangers and his pace, tight control and two good feet made him difficult to pin down. Chris Ball, at inside-right, was a worker who tackled powerfully and distributed intelligently; he was a goalscorer, too, who had found the net in the two previous rounds against Mansfield and Hartlepools.

At centre-forward Walsall had one of their enduring heroes, Gilbert Alsop, a man with dark hair, good, strong features and an easy air of independence. He took knocks and gave them, he could shoot venomously with each foot and never stopped running or trying – and to this day his consistency as a goal-scorer has never been matched by any Walsall player. In each of the two following seasons, 1933-4 and 1934-5, he scored forty League goals, which is still a club record. Bill Sheppard was Alsop's partner at inside-left, a new acquisition who had begun his career with Crook Town and progressed purposefully towards Fellows Park by way of Liverpool, Watford, Queen's Park Rangers and Coventry. On the left-wing, finally, there was Fred Lee who had also played for Coventry, a young, promising player who ran straight, centred well and was attracting the attention of other clubs.

This was the side that the great Herbert Chapman himself, manager of Arsenal and the first man of football, came to watch play Barnsley on the first Saturday of 1933. 'The Swift', of the *Walsall Times* watched the watcher: 'When Alsop scored in the first minute, Mr Chapman made a little note in his pocket-book and sat back with a smile! A large number of people would like to know what it was he scribbled down but I think I shall not be far wrong in surmising that Alsop will be well and truly watched in the opening minutes of the game — and the rest.'

Chapman, of course, could afford to smile at almost anyone and anything. This round and florid Yorkshireman was an honest-to-goodness legend in his own lifetime. He had built for Huddersfield the greatest team in their history, one capable of winning three League championships in a row, and then moved to Highbury in 1925 to start pushing Arsenal towards the same overwhelming achievement. They remain the only two clubs to have managed this hat-trick.

As a player with Tottenham, Chapman was never more than ordinary — remembered only for his flamboyant yellow boots — but as a manager he was years ahead of his time. He was a polished talker, a natural psychologist, a shrewd and tough businessman, a ruthless martinet but a good friend and understanding father-figure, a pioneer, a realist, a gambler, a confidence trickster, an inspired motivator and a publicist.

Chapman was one of the first men to insist on first-class facilities for spectators; he tried out numbered shirts five years before the idea was approved by the Football Association; he advocated white balls and all-weather pitches; he experimented with goal judges and independent time keeping; he had the name of the local underground station changed from Gillespie

Road to Arsenal; and nearly twenty years before the first official floodlit match was played in England, he championed the idea of playing football under artificial lighting. He held the first team-talks, used a table marked out like a pitch to illustrate his theories and encouraged his players to take part in frank discussion. Not surprisingly, too, he was the first manager to come to terms with the change in the offside law in 1925. He introduced the third back – the 'stopper' or the 'policeman' – once it was decided that only two defenders and not three needed to be between attacker and ball. It changed the role of the centre-half and the whole shape of the game.

Arsenal flourished and blossomed under Chapman. He established the right of the manager to be the central figure in a club; he demanded power, loyalty, total obedience, punctuality at all times and devotion to both club and profession. His players regarded him with a mixture of awe and respect – and, in return, Chapman was scrupulously fair and true to his word.

Above all Chapman was a builder of winning football teams. He knew exactly what he wanted in the way of method and ability. His method, which evolved with changing laws and trends, was not complex; a stopper between two full-backs marking wide, dual-purpose wing-halves who provided quickly and retreated quickly, a deep-lying inside-forward to feed two raiding wingers, and a centre-forward and inside-forward to score goals. It was Chapman's genius which made it work.

Chapman was prepared to spend hugely but he was also a sensitive and brave judge of young talent. Frank Moss was Oldham's reserve goalkeeper when Chapman spotted him, but once at Highbury he developed into an England international of the highest class, and he and Harry Hibbs of Birmingham were considered by their contemporaries to be the two best goalkeepers of the 1930s. George Male was an amateur centre-half with Clapham when Chapman signed him and he went on to win nineteen caps for England and to be recognized as the finest right-back of his time. Herbie Roberts, the shy, red-headed giant who became Chapman's prototype stopper, was signed from his home-town team, Oswestry, for just £200.

Cliff Bastin – 'Boy' Bastin on the left-wing – was only seventeen when Chapman paid Exeter £2,000 for him.

Chapman spotted him by accident – he had gone to watch another player – but saw in the young Devonian the elusiveness, the coolness and finishing power that was to win him every major honour before his twenty-first birthday. He scored thirty-three goals – a record for a winger – during the season in which Walsall beat Arsenal.

Chapman emphasized his willingness to invest even larger sums in proven quality of the highest class by buying Alex James from Preston for £9,000 in 1929 and, that same year, David Jack from Bolton for £10,890, the first five-figure transfer. The country raised its hands in horror at such extravagance; Chapman smiled at what he considered to be a couple of bargains. James, one of Scotland's famous 'Blue Devils', was an imp of a man with buttoned-down sleeves and baggy shorts. Jack of England, who has already figured in our story, was a tall and elegant man who elevated football to an art form. James created goals with wit and impudence. Jack scored them with charm and even something approaching good manners.

There were other equally celebrated and important members of the side, too, but they did not play against Walsall. A nasty epidemic of 'flu was floating about the country and, it was widely reported and accepted, three of Arsenal's regular squad were laid low during the week of the visit to Fellows Park. They were Bob John, their long-serving Welsh international left-half, Jack Lambert, a splendidly aggressive and consistent goal scorer, and Tim Coleman, another of their front-line strikers. Eddie Hapgood, captain of Arsenal and England and one of the game's most polished left-backs, was said to be injured and, to complicate things further, Joe Hulme was in the middle of a lean spell and had been dropped – Hulme, of England, a dashing and spectacular winger on his day, a free-scoring Middlesex batsman and a natural at almost every ball-game.

Chapman seemed to have one or two problems to solve, but Arsenal's resources were so great that it was hardly a crisis. The club used 22 players in winning the championship that season; and the 118 goals they scored in their 42 League games were shared by nine men.

Chapman's decision, however, was to call four men into the

side of whom only Norman Sidey, the tall reserve centre-half, had first-team experience. Sidey took John's place at left-half. Tommy Black, who had just joined the club from a Scottish junior team, deputized for Hapgood at left-back, and Billy Warnes and Charlie Walsh completed the attack.

Warnes was an amateur international who had come from Woking, an Isthmian League club, a clever but lightweight player who had no stomach for the kind of demolishing tackles they knew were waiting for them at Walsall. Walsh, for his part, believed he was the best centre-forward on Arsenal's books. Chapman was not so convinced – but he decided that this was the moment to give Walsh the chance to prove that his ability was the equal of his confidence.

Arsenal still had seven internationals in their side, Moss, Male, Roberts, Jack, James, Bastin and 'Tiger' Hill of Scotland, a tenacious little man, at right-half. But, as we shall discover, Chapman's decision to play Black, Warnes and Walsh proved to be the biggest – and perhaps only disastrous – mistake of his career.

Nevertheless, Arsenal prepared for Walsall as diligently as if they were meeting one of their First Division contemporaries at Wembley itself. The previous Saturday they had played at Sunderland and, in their own royal manner, they left Roker Park immediately after the game. Police motorcyclists cleared the roads as they dashed to a town forty miles away where the Flying Scotsman made an unscheduled stop just for them – a piece of enterprise which got the party into Kings Cross at ten o'clock that evening instead of in the early hours of Sunday morning.

Arsenal spent the week at Brighton, their customary away-from-it-all spot before every Cup-tie, while Walsall stayed at home, sampled the brine baths at Droitwich, played a round or two of golf and – entering into the spirit of things – gathered in the middle of their pitch to eat some oysters. The build-up to the match was something they relished. Their chance relationship with Arsenal had made them into a subject of national interest, and they savoured every moment.

The papers enjoyed themselves, emphasizing the differences between the clubs. One made the point that Arsenal spent more on their boots, £87, than Walsall had spent on their team. Another claimed that 'Walsall's men eat fish and chips and drink beer' and that the mascot of their team was a little silver cup inscribed 'The Beer-Shifters Challenge Cup'. H.L. Fellows, Walsall's chairman, the man who gave his name to the ground and who was devoted to the club, replied sharply: 'It may be that some of our players have an occasional pint of beer, and they may also, occasionally, eat fish and chips but we treat this kind of story with the contempt it deserves.'

Walsall anticipated a full house of 26,000 spectators – 8,000 more than the club's record – and extended the banking on the popular side of the ground and improved the enclosure in front of the main stand. They made the game all-ticket, raised prices all round and decided the gates would be opened at noon, two and a half hours before the kick-off. A fund was started to provide two-shilling terrace tickets for the unemployed, and the local magistrates granted thirty-four pubs in the town an extra two hours' opening time on the day of the match.

The crowd, in the event, proved disappointingly small, 11,149, with the inflow of Arsenal supporters a long way below expectations. Trains from the capital were only half full and coaches few in number. Extra police were on duty but they had little to do. There was no late rush and everything was nice and orderly.

There were several reasons for the modest crowd. The result, for one thing, was taken for granted and Arsenal's supporters in particular felt disinclined to waste time and money on the inevitable. Many local people, anticipating a packed ground, decided they would not risk the crush and they also resented Walsall's decision to raise prices. The club's curious answer was that the increases were necessary to stop them being overwhelmed by applications. It certainly did that.

Nobody, anywhere, gave Walsall a chance. The *Birmingham Sports Argus* summed up the general feeling: 'There is such a vast difference in the merits of the sides that the result seems inevitable, but curious things happen in Cup ties. Really, I don't think it will happen at Fellows Park, but you never know. Walsall have decided upon a plan of campaign. If they are permitted to put it into practice they might surprise their famous rivals, but I cannot see the intelligent players of Arsenal being led into a trap. Which, in other words, means that they will win.'

Mr Fellows went into the home dressing-room before the game and told the Walsall team he had just re-read the Bible story of how David killed Goliath. 'I didn't actually see that victory', he said, 'but I'm hoping to see another version from you.' The team bellowed back that he would. They were even more taken with the gesture of another director who offered them, privately, a bonus of £5 each if they won – a sizeable sum set against their weekly wage of £6 a man.

Next door in the visitors' dressing-room, meanwhile, there was an early indication that at least one member of the Arsenal team was having trouble with his nerves. Herbert Chapman was having a last word with his players and to Walsh, the cocky young man who was getting his big chance, he said: 'Good luck son, I want you to show me just what you can do.' 'Count on me', replied Walsh, 'I'm going to play the game of my life.' 'You'll do, lad', said Chapman – and, as he turned away, he added: 'By the way, you'd better put your stockings on unless you want to give the crowd a laugh.' Walsh had put his boots on over his ordinary socks.

The Walsall players were secret witnesses to some of what was going on in the Arsenal dressing-room. Only a wooden partition separated the two teams and at one point there was a gap through which they could peep. They noticed, with some glee, that the great Alex James was so small he had to stand on a bench to reach his peg.

Outside, in the centre circle, the Aldridge Colliery Band was doing its hearty best. 'Pack Up Your Troubles' it played, and some of the crowd even started singing; but the song died quickly because a Black Country crowd is dour and rather phlegmatic. They cheer when they have something worthwhile to cheer, but not before. Their moment was to come.

Fellows Park must have looked a daunting place to Arsenal as they took the field. The small pitch was hemmed in tight by the crowd and all the way along one end was the wall of a laundry topped by a wire net. The net stopped wayward shots finishing on the railway line to Birmingham. Arsenal must have noticed, too, that the Walsall team looked tall, sturdy and menacingly determined.

Walsall won the toss and, on a soft pitch that looked certain to cut up, the teams lined up like this: *Walsall* – Cunningham; Bennett, Bird; Reed, Leslie, Salt; Coward, Ball, Alsop, Sheppard and Lee. *Arsenal* – Moss; Male, Black; Hill, Roberts, Sidey; Warne, Jack, Walsh, James to Bastin.

Arsenal were prepared for Walsall to start with devilish aggression and they were not disappointed. The First Division team were awarded ten free-kicks in as many minutes. Roberts received a badly cut eye the first time he went up for the ball, Bastin was flattened by Bennett the first time he got possession on the left-wing and James was twice sent spinning to the ground. A less lenient referee than Mr A. Taylor from Wigan might have sent off two or three Walsall players and changed the course of history.

There was no mistaking the more skilful side. James kept getting up off his backside to remind everyone that he was the supreme craftsman, Bastin flickered into life on the left and Jack looked manifestly superior. There were chances, too, but the attack which had been terrorizing the best defences in the country – 76 goals in 25 games in the First Division, 17 more than any other club – had for once lost its teeth.

Walsall had everything going for them – including the unfortunate Charlie Walsh. The young Arsenal centre-forward was wildly over-eager and not only managed to squander all his own chances, once misjudging a perfect centre from Bastin so utterly that the ball hit him on a shoulder, but succeeded in confounding his own colleagues as well. He made one prodigious leap to reach another centre from Bastin, just as the unmarked David Jack was picking his spot in the Walsall net. The centre had been intended for Jack who looked certain to score. Walsh's effort sent the ball yards wide and for a moment Gentleman Jack had murder in his eyes.

Chapman even switched Jack and Walsh around at half-time, Jack becoming centre-forward, and in the early part of the second-half they had their best spell. The balance of the game had changed and it seemed only a matter of time before mind would triumph over muscle.

Right on the hour, however, destiny took over. Lee swung across a corner from Walsall's left and Alsop's timing in the middle was perfect: his header beat Moss, and Fellows Park suddenly realized the impossible was looking distinctly possible. The roar told everyone in Walsall what had happened.

It was a moment which Alsop was still remembering clearly nearly fifty years later in the season of the 100th Cup Final. 'I didn't make proper contact with the ball', he recalled. 'It just seemed to glide off my head into the net, just as if the ball knew where it wanted to go, and even now I still feel and taste the elation as the crowd roared and the rest of the team mobbed me.' Alsop, a diamond of a centre-forward, endlessly aggressive and competitive, later became groundsman at Fellows Park. He was alive and well, living in Walsall and watching every home match, as the 1980s picked up pace.

The goal gave Walsall new lungs and fresh limbs. Cunningham was inspired, Bennett and Bird tackled and covered relentlessly, Reed and Salt were tireless, and Leslie was indestructible. They took the shortest route at all times and Arsenal players were merely obstructions to be demolished and cleared out of their path.

The second decisive moment of the match soon followed: a penalty to Walsall who, ironically, had been conceding free-kicks with metronomic regularity. Black, Arsenal's left-back, deliberately kicked Alsop – an act of bitter frustration. 'For a moment there was dead silence', reported the *Walsall Times*. 'Then there was a hub-bub of yelling and shouting. Ball made the first move of the players and when he saw the still form of his colleague on the ground he rushed at Black. Soon a whole crowd of players, both avengers and peace-makers, were in a struggling mass. The referee seemed almost as dumbfounded as everyone else, but he quickly restored order and made the only possible decision – a penalty against Arsenal.' Sheppard, Walsall's spot-kick expert, was marvelously cool. His shot was wickedly hard and low, and wide of Moss in the Arsenal goal: Walsall 2, Arsenal 0. A nearby factory chimney chose that moment to throw huge clouds of grey-black smoke into the air and the pitch, for a minute or two, was a thing of misty unreality. So, for Arsenal, was the match.

The moment that Mr Taylor ended the match the crowd broke over the palings, caught three or four of the Walsall players and chaired them around the pitch. They cheered everyone and everything. This was a Black Country crowd with something to celebrate.

Inside, the Mayor of Walsall, Councillor W. Dean, was telling anyone who would lend him an ear: 'This is the greatest day of my life.' The Arsenal dressing-room was somewhat less ecstatic. Bastin, in his autobiography *Cliff Bastin Remembers,* was to write:

> We certainly were an unhappy team as we changed slowly and moodily. It was all the more infuriating because we knew we ought to have won. True, the Walsall players had at times behaved more like steam-rollers than footballers. True, Charlie Walsh and Billy Warnes had been misfits. Nevertheless, granting all this, we had still been presented with enough chances to have won.
>
> Never have I seen Herbert Chapman look so miserably unhappy. He made a brave, desperate but unavailing effort to cheer us all up. 'Never mind, boys', he said, 'these things do happen.' But we were all inconsolable and so, for that matter, was he. I think he felt the blow more than any of us. Here was the team which he had come to when it was struggling pathetically at the bottom of the First Division; the team which he had made one of the greatest in the history of football, beaten by a fifth-rate side. Napoleon must have felt like that in Russia, a hundred and twenty-one years before.

It was a totally new experience for Chapman and his immediate reactions were erratic. He was asked by a Walsall councillor if he had a message for the Council. 'Get your rates down', replied the great man. A few minutes later, asked a less eccentric question, he answered: 'There is no excuse for us. On the day Walsall deserved to win. There is just one thing that might be said, and that is how much we regret the incident of the penalty in the second-half. I'm particularly sorry that should have happened.'

Chapman never spoke lightly. Black was transferred to Plymouth within a week and, as if Chapman was trying to erase the memory of Walsall, Walsh was sold to Brentford within a month and Warnes moved to Norwich at the end of the season. Of the four reserves Chapman put into his side at Fellows Park, only Sidey was allowed to remain.

There is no doubt, however, that Chapman himself was largely to blame for the defeat. Bob Wall, who was to become the club's much-respected General Secretary and later a director, was Chapman's young assistant at the time, and sometime before his death early in 1981 he told me:

> Herbert made the biggest mistake of his life. All the players he left out could have played. There is no doubt about that. But Herbert decided that as we were playing Walsall he was going to take a gamble and, as he put it, 'give the kids a chance'. It didn't work and afterwards in the dressing room I heard him say to our trainer Tom Whittaker: 'We made a blunder today, Tom, but nobody is going to know it.'
>
> A few minutes later I walked into the Walsall Board-room with him, he put out his hand and said 'Congratulations, the best team won.' You can imagine my feelings. A great man. I knew just how he felt. I knew what was in his mind but he could still take it on the chin and put out his hand.

Arsenal left the ground, quietly, unobtrusively, but not before David Jack had gone to Walsall's dressing-room and congratulated them. The North London Club's fans trooped disconsolately down Hilary Street, but at other League grounds, in Boardroom and on terrace, there were cheers. The country shared Walsall's pleasure. At Highbury, where Arsenal's reserves were playing, everyone burst out laughing. They thought it was a leg-pull. Then the message was confirmed, and reconfirmed, and they looked as if they would never laugh again.

The game did not provide the expected financial windfall. Publicans did well enough but trade in the local shops was poor. The receipts for the game itself amounted to £1,487 13s 6d, which, in the end, left each club with £589 16s 6d. But this was not a day to be measure in such a dull, material way.

'The Swift' of the *Walsall Times,* for example, knew as he sat down to tackle his match report that something special was required of him.

Is it true? Is it not a dream that I shall awake and smile at? No! Even now I cannot quite grasp that my little Walsall – the team I gaze upon so anxiously every week – has had the cheek, the impudence, to wipe the great and mighty Arsenal out of the English Cup and send them back to the Metropolis bewailing a whipping at the hands of an insignificant club in the Northern Section of the Third Division. And yet – it must be true, for I saw them with my eyes – I watched Alsop and Sheppard do the things that made their names famous throughout the football world – heard the mighty roars that followed these actions. Indeed, did I not so far forget my complete impartiality as to give vocal praise as the Saddlers left the field – triumphant!

Dreams, alas, are only true while they last. Walsall's dream was ended by Manchester City at Maine Road in the next round. Walsall sent the same team and 6,000 supporters north but two goals by Eric Brook, one in each half, the first scrappy, the second a beauty, were too much for the little team from the Black Country. A crowd of 52,085 gathered to bid farewell to Walsall and their cheers rang with sincerity. It was a dignified exit.

Walsall finished fifth in the northern section of the Third Division and Arsenal, their pride badly bruised but their momentum still quickening, went on to win the League championship by a margin of four points. They won it the following year by three points and again the following year by four. They dominated the 1930s, before and after the sudden death of Chapman early in 1934, winning the League title in 1931, 1933, 1934, 1935 and 1938 and the Cup in 1930 and 1936. That is the measure of Walsall's achievement.

It took an Arsenal supporter with a sense of humour to sum it all up:

Sing a song of Walsall
  Of an English football tie,
How eleven sturdy local men
  Made an Arsenal captain sigh.

What a rollicking lot of Roysters,
  Good fellows in Fellows Park,
Who spiked their guns with oysters,
  Wasn't it a lark?

Darwen – 'the first of the iconoclasts'. Back row (left to right): J. Duxbury, S. Fish, W. Brindle, L. Broughton, W.H. Moorhouse. Middle row: T. Marshall, T. Rostron, Dr Gledhill, Dr J.C. Holden, R. Kirkham, T. Bury. Front row: F. Suter. Brindle and Marshall are wearing England shirts. *(Howard Peters.)*

Victorian Darwen – 'a place of tight, little streets and dark, Satanic mills'. A rare picture showing Darwen FC's old ground at Barley Bank. *(Howard Peters.)*

Two photographs from a contemporary edition of the *Illustrated London News* which reported the Tottenham *v.* Sheffield United match. *Above:* A section of the Crystal Palace crowd before the 1901 Cup Final – the biggest gate, 114,000, football had known. *Below:* The kick-off of the 1901 Cup Final. 'The south was challenging the north . . . there was a huge sense of occasion about this day.' *(Mansell Collection.)*

The Cup Final of 1901 at the Crystal Palace. Tottenham 2, Sheffield United 2. Centre: a strong run by Spurs outside-right Tom Smith. Top left: Sandy Brown scores Spurs' second goal. Bottom right: George Clawley, Spurs' goalkeeper, avoids a 'rush' by United's Walter Bennett. *(BBC Hulton Picture Library.)*

Swindon of the Southern League score their winning goal against Everton, the Cup favourites, in the quarter-finals of 1912. Billy Scott, Everton's goalkeeper, is on his knees. *(BBC Hulton Picture Library.)*

Caps, bowlers and mud. Swindon 2, Everton 1 . . . 'The pride of Swindon's townspeople in their football team was boundless.' *(BBC Hulton Picture Library.)*

Hubert Pearson, the West Bromwich Albion goalkeeper, saves a Charlton shot in the third round of 1923 – but Albion were one of three First Division clubs beaten by Charlton. *(BBC Hulton Picture Library.)*

Freddy Wood, Charlton's goalkeeper, punches clear from David Jack, the Bolton and England inside-right, in their quarter-final at the Valley. But Jack had the last word: Charlton 0, Jack 1. *(BBC Hulton Picture Library.)*

Walsall after their famous victory over Arsenal in 1933. Back row: Bird, Reed, Bennett, H. Waite (trainer), Cunningham, J. Wilson (assistant secretary), Leslie, Salt, Sheppard (scorer of the second goal, a penalty). Middle row: W. Slade (secretary-manager), E. Jackson (director), H. Fellows (chairman), Mrs Dean (mayoress), W. Dean (mayor), H. Lake and A. Eyre (directors). Front row: Coward, Ball, Alsop (scorer of first goal), Lee. *(Colorsport.)*

Sixty-four numbered balls and a velvet bag wait for the third-round draw in 1935 – the first draw to be broadcast. 'One of the FA Cup's most compelling quarter-hours.' *(Central Press.)*

The beginning of the end of Yeovil's famous Cup run. A crowd of 81,000 saw Manchester United beat them 8-0. Right to left: Johnny Carey (Manchester United), referee Alf Bond Yeovil's mascot Rex Rainey, and player-manager Alec Stock. *(Sunday Express.)*

Dickie Dyke, Yeovil's goalkeeper, forces the ball away during the Southern League club's victory over Sunderland in 1949. Dyke, a twenty-three-year-old Sunday-school teacher, was playing in his second first-team game. *(Press Association.)*

Norwich City's goalkeeper Ken Nethercott, his right shoulder dislocated, punches clear with his one good arm in their 1959 quarter-final with Sheffield United at Bramall Lane. The Sheffield centre-forward is Derek Pace. *(Press Association.)*

Norwich City fans at Tottenham in 1959. 'White Hart Lane was turned into a corner of Norfolk.' *(Press Association.)*

Tony Jones, unmarked, scores his second goal for Oxford United against Blackburn Rovers in the fifth round, 1964. Mike England (left) looks on. Oxford won 3-1. *(Press Association.)*

Oxford celebrate their victory over Blackburn. 'The gold shirts of Oxford disappeared without trace until Ron Atkinson, their captain, was suddenly lifted up, a flash of colour above the bobbing heads.' *(Press Association.)*

Ray Crawford of Colchester, lying on the ground, hooks his second goal past Gary Sprake, the Leeds goalkeeper, and Jack Charlton. 1971: Colchester 3, Leeds 2. *(Press Association.)*

Dick Graham, manager of Colchester, is hugged by his players after their fifth-round victory over Leeds – a gesture of affection and respect which Graham admitted 'touched me ridiculously'. *(Press Association.)*

Peter Rogers (number 8) scores the third of Exeter's four goals against Newcastle in the fifth round, 1981. 'Exeter were inspired under their own floodlights, their fans thunderously behind them.' *(Press Association.)*

Tony Kellow, Exeter's leading scorer, shoots wide from the bottom of a scrum at White Hart Lane. Exeter, the last giant killers of the first hundred tournaments, are on their way out . . . and Tottenham are on their way to victory at Wembley. *(Sport & General Press Agency.)*

6 Yeovil...1949

The grand and ugly city of Manchester chose a sullen afternoon in February 1949 to remove all lingering doubts about the affection which football has for its giant killers.

A crowd of 81,565 assembled to watch Manchester United, the most celebrated team in all the land, destroy a side of part-time players from the green and gentle acres of Somerset by eight goals to nil. It was achieved and accepted without embarrassment, and the cheers that rolled like thunder around the ground at the end were for the little men who had dared. It was a warm-hearted tribute to a marvellous flight of fancy.

They were moments the countrymen of Yeovil Town would dearly have liked to preserve, on film, in file, on canvas, or even in bottles. They knew, in the privacy of their dressing-room, that they had earned themselves an indelible place in the history of the game.

They were a non-League club who had reached the fifth round of the FA Cup and, along the way, captured the respect of the whole nation with conviction and style. They had beaten Lovells Athletic, Romford, Weymouth, Bury of the Second Division, and Sunderland of the First, who were known with explicit good reason as 'the Bank of England Club'. Their 2-1 victory over Sunderland, above all, has become the stuff of legend. It was an astonishing achievement which year by year is still acquiring new colour and depth. It is a story, too, of Yeovil's famous sloping pitch at Huish – the 'Boot Hill' of football, the 'strip with the dip', the 'pitch with the hitch'.

Yeovil were then in the less fashionable half of the Southern League – with 14 points from 19 games. Their players were an interesting but rather motley collection who cost the club £65 a week in wages. A few weeks before the bookmakers were quoting them at 5,000 to 1 for the Cup. Sunderland had been members of the First Division since 1890, won the League championship six times, finished runners-up on five occasions and won the Cup in 1937. Their history was adorned with great names and achievements; they belonged to a corner of the kingdom where football was in the bloodstream. They were also the biggest spenders in the game. Their team in 1949 had been put together at a cost of nearly £60,000 – a sum which had people inside as well as outside the game shaking their heads in disbelief.

On paper it looked to be no match at all; on grass it proved to be a game which enriched the story of football.

It was almost more than the town of Yeovil could take in at a time when the shadow of the Second World War was still sharp and dark. They were days of economy and utility, of high hopes but short supply. Yeovil itself was a quiet, unassuming market town of less than 23,000 people, a place of broad accents and generous hearts, in the south-eastern corner of Somerset. Railway lines ran into it from five different directions and, having been spared the serious attentions of the Luftwaffe, it was getting on nicely with the business of producing beer, food and gloves.

The town's football club was little more remarkable. It was formed in 1920 by amalgamating Yeovil Casuals and Petters United and, soon afterwards, it accepted the challenge of semi-professionalism and the Southern League. The club had reached the third round of the Cup on three occasions before the war and won its fair share of silverware on other, less celebrated levels.

Yeovil Town, in short, was a small club in a small town; it had ambition and drive but there was no hint early in the 1948-49 season of the audacious deeds to come. Even the Cup-run itself began unpromisingly. They were drawn away to Lovells Athletic, a Newport club with a side of worth and experience, in the fourth qualifying round – and Lovells, playing direct and well-ordered football, took a two-goal lead. Lovells had an outstanding centre-half in Harry Clarke who was soon to help Arthur Rowe's Spurs win the League championship in 1951 and later to play for England. He was 6ft 3ins tall and the central pillar of a Lovells' defence which seemed quite capable of holding Yeovil at arm's length.

Yeovil needed help from someone and it came, unexpectedly,

from another member of the Lovells' defence. He tried to pass the ball smoothly back to his goalkeeper from fifteen yards out but mishit it, fiercely, and the ball zipped into the roof of his own net; a fine, unstoppable shot. Yeovil equalized soon after and, in a game of exciting but uneven quality, they went on to win by 3-2. A crowd of 1,200 turned on its heel convinced – not feeling too sorry about it – that they had heard the last of Yeovil.

The first and second rounds proper were negotiated with ease. Romford, at home, and Weymouth, away, were each beaten by four goals to nil, and Yeovil now found themselves in more exalted company. The third-round draw gave them a home tie against Bury, who immediately emphasized their worth by beating West Bromwich Albion, the Second Division leaders. Bury had a young and skilful side and doubted Yeovil's ability to last the pace.

It was not an opinion, however, shared by Alec Stock, Yeovil's player-manager and a man who, with astuteness, honesty and example, was to play an outstanding part in his club's success and launch himself on a remarkable career. He and his trainer Stan Abbott, a former Yeovil player and one of the club's best-loved figures, went to watch Bury at the first possible opportunity. They decided the Second Division club could be beaten by quick distribution and long, early passes to the wings.

Stock was an uncommonly interesting and versatile chap. He was a man of Somerset, compact in build, popular, intelligent and highly articulate. He understood men as well as football. He was ambitious but a respecter of tradition, hard but forgiving, shrewd but generous, a realist but also a romantic. He had, too, the ability to make people believe in him. Here, instinctively, was a man they felt they could trust.

He had played for Charlton and Queen's Park Rangers before the war, served with distinction in the Royal Armoured Corps during it – a period in which he learnt a great deal about man-management – and then in 1946, at the age of twenty-seven, he joined Yeovil as the youngest player-manager in the country. There were more than sixty applicants for the job, among them Cliff Bastin, but the comparatively unknown

Stock impressed most of all.

It was an inspired choice because Stock took charge. He *was* the club – player, manager, coach, public-relations man, purse-keeper, clerk and groundsman's help-mate, 'Player managership', he would say, 'is violent exercise on top of a pile of worries.'

Stock was at the beginning of a managerial career which was to take him to Leyton Orient, Arsenal, A.S. Roma, Queen's Park Rangers, Luton, Fulham and Bournemouth – a journey of achievement, adventure and lasting friendships. He even gave Queen's Park Rangers the distinction of becoming the first Third Division club to win a major Wembley final – the League Cup Final of 1967, in which they beat West Bromwich Albion by 3-2 after being two goals down at half-time. He was that rarest of all kinds of manager, a survivor, and he retired as the father-figure of his profession after thirty-five years in the firing-line to live in a lovely thatched cottage in Dorset.

Certainly Yeovil could not have had a better man to handle the tidal wave of publicity which rolled over them early in 1949. Stock did not merely cope with the situation; he revelled in it. 'The Press put us under a microscope', he remembers.

> They examined us, analysed us and lived with us. They pulled us apart and put us together again. I had one call from Jack Milligan, a reporter on the old Daily Graphic. He was after a new angle and while we were talking the subject of our slope cropped up. Nothing much had ever been written about it but I thought 'Why not?' and gave him the facts – the way the slope dipped, its 10 foot drop and so on. Next morning the Graphic announced to the world that the pitch sloped 14 feet from one side to the other and in the next few days every other reporter seemed to add a couple of feet to its steepness. By the time match-day came round everyone must have had the idea we played on the north face of the Eiger.
>
> I was at my desk on the morning of the game when our groundsman put his head round the door. 'Bury have just arrived', he said. 'I looked out of the window and there they were, out on the pitch, bending down every other step to have a look at this fearsome slope they'd read about. I knew most of them would go away convinced they'd need rope and

mountaineering boots to get through the game. One up to us.'

Yeovil's players did not take kindly to suggestions that the slope was a secret weapon but Stock, never less than honest, admits it had its uses. 'It always helped to know just how to play our pitch', he recalls. 'We used to keep on banging the ball up the slope, to the winger on the top side, because if it was played the other way it was always likely to pick up too much pace. The winger on the top side could just blow his crosses over. Mind you, it was hard work for those at the bottom of the slope but it was toughest of all for opponents who did not rumble what was going on.'

Stock's team, like many unconsidered trifles before and since who have surprised more celebrated opposition, was not short of ability or experience. They were pictured in many newspapers as being country bumpkins, smock-wearers with straw in their mouths, but this was selling them short. Few would have claimed to be world-beaters but many had played the game at a respectable level.

Stan Hall, Yeovil's goalkeeper, a tall, brave man, had played for Finchley, the London amateur club, before turning professional for Clapton Orient (rechristened Leyton Orient in 1946). Arthur Hickman – 'Big Hearted Arthur' – was a solid and reliable right-back who had joined Aston Villa straight from school and guested for Raith Rovers, Fulham and Glentoran during the war. His full-back partner, Ralph Davis, a local glove cutter, had guested for Hereford and was regarded as one of the hardest tacklers in the Southern League.

Bob Keeton was a tough but constructive right-half who lasted the full ninety minutes of every game and who had played for Torquay and, during the war, Brentford, Fulham and Crystal Palace. Les Blizzard was considered to be one of the best centre-halves in the Southern League, a lean 25-year-old who had a passion for fish and chips; he had played for Queen's Park Rangers and Bournemouth, and was again attracting the attention of League clubs. Nick Collins, at left-half, was one of the most popular members of the team; he was also a wing-half who could attack enterprisingly and defend stubbornly. He captained Crystal Palace for several years before the war but had settled in Yeovil and ran the Wellington Inn just a minute from the ground. 'Life at the Wellington', he liked to claim, 'is all beer and skittles' – but on the field he chose to make it a very earnest business indeed.

Bob Hamilton, on the right-wing, was only twenty-three but he had played seventy-one League games in two seasons for Chester and was a quick, elusive forward who could play on either flank. Alec Stock was as lively an inside-right as he was a manager; he was full of ideas and movement and the architect of many of their best moments.

Eric Bryant, their centre-forward, was at the peak of his form, a hard-running, hard-shooting leader who had scored twice in each of the three earlier rounds. Before joining Yeovil he had scored regularly for Mansfield in the Third Division North and before that he had played a lot of inter-Service football while serving with the RAF in India. Bryant kept himself fit by humping sacks of corn for a local merchant. The biggest man in the attack was Ray Wright who stood over six foot and was a deliberate but crafty inside-left who had been with Wolves and Exeter: he was the 'brain' of the side. Jack Hargreaves, on the left-wing, was a former Leeds and Bristol City player who centred accurately and was also dangerous when cutting inside.

It was certainly a good enough side to persuade 13,500 people that the result was not a foregone conclusion. Special trains and coaches brought fans into the town from all corners of the west country and there were queues outside the ground four hours before the kick-off. Among dozens of good-luck gifts and messages was a sprig of white heather from Dave Halliday, who had managed Yeovil before the war when they first began to make a name for themselves as Cup-fighters. Halliday, a former Dundee, Sunderland, Arsenal and Manchester City forward, had left Yeovil to take over at Aberdeen and later managed Leicester City.

Inside the ground spectators perched on buildings, walls, hoardings and trees and Bury, led by their captain Leslie Hart, were given a real Somerset welcome. A few seconds later Yeovil came out, led by Master Rex Rainey, their ten-year-old-mascot, and the volume of the cheering seemed to double. The cameras of Gaumont British News were there: the people of Yeovil knew they were playing to a national audience.

The game itself was exciting but the issue was never in doubt. Bury were a curious mixture of nerves and complacency, and Yeovil, physically and mentally tough, won by 3-1. They ran their League opponents to a standstill and finished much the fresher side. Hickman and Davis hit long, accurate balls out of defence, Blizzard had the beating of Dave Massart, Bury's powerful and much publicized 'hat-trick king', and in front there was so much mobility and determination that the Second Division side were never allowed to settle down. Bury might have been embarrassed even more but for their athletic goal-keeper, Ken Grieves, the tall Lancashire and Australian cricketer.

Yeovil took the lead in the seventh minute when Grieves did well to stop a shot but couldn't hold the ball and Hargreaves moved quickly at the far post to head in. Massart, eluding Blizzard for the first and just about only time, equalized after nineteen minutes with a full-blooded drive off the underside of the bar – and for a few minutes, with their 5ft 5in left-winger Alf Bellis in lively form, Bury threatened to take hold of the game. It was a phase which soon passed and Yeovil took the lead again just before half-time when Bryant set things up nicely for Wright who was having a fine game. Bury clearly did not relish the battle; they began to look dejected, their play too close and too fussy, and it was Bryant again with a strong, aggressive run who prepared the way for Hamilton to score Yeovil's third, mid-way through the second-half.

The celebrations started immediately and the crowd did not even begin to filter away until an hour later when Stock spoke to them over the loudspeakers. He thanked them for their support and encouragement – and only then did the party move on. It was opening time.

Yeovil were in the fourth round for the first time and the only non-League club left in the Cup. There was a sense of mighty occasion and huge expectation when the draw was made – and everyone's wildest hopes were realized. Yeovil were drawn at home to Sunderland! Bury had been one thing; but this was something else. Sunderland kept company with the Gods on Mount Olympus.

Sunderland were a club which mattered: their pedigree was impeccable, the roll of men who had played for them included many of the legendary figures of the game, among them Hugh Wilson, Jimmy Millar, Alf Common, George Holley, Charlie Buchan, Warnie Cresswell and Raich Carter, and their supporters were among the most partisan, most loyal and most knowledgeable in football. They were also, of course, a permanent fixture in the First Division; they never even considered the possibility of relegation. There was dignity in the name, distinction in the style, no horizon to their ambitions.

The team Sunderland prepared carefully for the visit to Yeovil had cost nearly £60,000 to build, with a third of that, a record at the time, invested in Len Shackleton. He was a rebel, an eccentric, a showman and a celebrity; his gifts were boundless and his range complete. He was an inside-left who could mesmerize opponents and delight crowds with his exquisite control and quick mind; but he could also exasperate and even anger on days when the sweat of the game seemed to offend him. But no one was ever indifferent to Shackleton who, before Roker Park, had played for Bradford Park Avenue and Newcastle. He won five caps for England; other men with less than half his talent have won fifty.

Around him Shackleton had a team capable of beating anyone in their day. It included seven men born within fifty miles of Sunderland and two members of the side which had won the Cup in 1937 – Johnny Mapson, the goalkeeper, and Len Duns at outside-right. Mapson was a Liverpudlian, a pinch under six foot, robustly built and splendidly reliable but often rather unorthodox. Duns was a Geordie who had played his first game for Sunderland a year before Mapson, in 1935, but was still progressive, still adventurous and still effective.

Sunderland had yet another celebrity at right-half, Willie Watson, for whom they paid Huddersfield £7,500 in 1946. He was one of those rare birds, an England international at both football and cricket. In his early days he played on the wing or at inside-forward, but he had settled down at right-half for Sunderland and was an astute and stylish influence. He was even more accomplished at cricket, a left-handed batsman of brilliance and tenacity for Yorkshire and England.

Jack Stelling, Sunderland's right-back, came from Washington just down the road, a little place with a splendid record for producing fine footballers, and was a busy and fearless player. Arthur Hudgell, an £8,000 signing from Crystal Palace, was his regular partner but he was unfit for the game against Yeovil and his place at left-back was taken by Barney Ramsden who had been a regular member of the Liverpool side and was hard, confident and quite prepared to mix things if the going got tough. Liverpool let him go with reluctance for £7,500.

Fred Hall, another County Durham man, captained the side with authority at centre-half – he had come from Blackburn for £6,000 – and Arthur Wright, on his left, was an attacking wing-half who had played his first game for the club in 1938 and later represented the Football League.

Jackie Robinson, Sunderland's inside-right, was a Northumberland man who had won four England caps before the war and been signed from Sheffield Wednesday for £6,500. Ronnie Turnbull was a dashing centre-forward, a native of Blyth, who was bought from Dundee for £9,000 and made his mark by scoring four goals against Portsmouth in his first game at Roker Park. Tommy Reynolds was the smallest man in the side, only 5ft 4in, but his speed and close-skills along the left wing had spoilt many a full-back's Saturday afternoon. He had been recommended to Sunderland while serving in Ceylon.

The whole of Somerset seemed determined to see the game. Applications for tickets were delivered daily by special Post Office vans. Ivan Rendall, Yeovil's 21-year-old secretary, and his schoolboy brother, converted a bedroom in their home in Rosebery Avenue into an office to deal with all the correspondence. Clearly there was not going to be room for everybody, and many regular supporters in local factories and workshops began complaining they were being frozen out. 'The trouble', said Rendall, 'is that 35,000 want to obtain admission to a ground which is limited to 15,000.'

Dark rumours circulated that a syndicate had bought thousands of tickets and intended making a fat killing a few hours before the kick-off. There were cat-calls and angry scuffles outside the ground and in the town. One group even rushed the ticket-office and police had to be called. Sunderland were sent 2,000 tickets – and within a few days they received a thousand applications from the Yeovil area.

Yeovil wonderd how they could increase the accommodation. They thought of putting up a temporary stand of tubular scaffolding, but the cost (£300) was considered prohibitive. They compromised by lining up hundreds of beer crates as extra seats. Prices, they had already decided, would be increased. Ground tickets remained at two shillings but enclosure seats – the beer crates! – were raised to 7s 6d and stand seats to a hefty 10s 6d. 'One thing puzzles me', said Stock. 'Our average gate is just over 3,000 . . . where do the other 11,000 get to each week?'

Sunderland, meantime, were having mixed feelings about it all. Bill Murray, their manager, said: 'It could be worse, but not much.' The bookmakers were suddenly a little less generous. Yeovil's odds were cut from 5,000 to 1 to 500 to 1. Other people were also getting in on the act. Down at the Pavilion Theatre at Bournemouth a comedian wearing a huge green and white Yeovil rosette told his audience: 'Roses are red, violets are blue – Sunderland 1, Yeovil 2.' He proved to be a fair judge.

Yeovil's players took the week off from work, enjoyed the brine baths at Weston-super-Mare, visited one or two local beauty spots, Bridport, Abbotsbury, Seaton and Beer, drank some sherry, ate some dates – and, minute by minute, were wound up by Stock. The town itself was in carnival mood. Shops were full of green and white and there were even pictures of Sunderland draped in red and white. The game was played in advance and in detail in every pub and cafe. The weather, the slope, the crowd and the players were chewed over with relish.

Sunderland arrived at the Manor Hotel in Yeovil on the Thursday before the match to find they had just missed a warm reception. On the way in they passed a fire-engine which had been dealing with a chimney fire. Next day they were allowed to train on the cinder track in front of the stand at Huish but not on the pitch itself. Yeovil's long-serving chairman, Bert Smith, admitted quite happily: 'We make no secret of the fact that the slope is a definite advantage to us and we would be foolish to let opponents of the calibre of Sunderland get the feel of it.'

Sunderland were not too worried; their football had got them safely through on Crewe's cramped ground in the previous round. They just wanted to loosen up.

It was a long trek for Sunderland's supporters, a round trip of more than 600 miles, which cost more than half a week's wages. A few cut their travelling down to two hours by spending £10 on a seat in a twin-engined aircraft. For most it involved a road journey of more than twelve hours and some, in coaches, did not arrive in Yeovil until long after the kick-off.

Every policeman in the area was drafted in and the precaution proved a wise one. Fans began to arrive before daybreak, many without tickets, and queues were already forming by eight o'clock. By the time the gates opened at noon the main queue was six deep and half a mile long. The police had to clear a passage for the teams when they arrived.

Yeovil had been obliged to make one change in their side. Stan Hall, their goalkeeper, was injured and his place was taken by Dickie Dyke, a 23-year-old amateur who worked in a solicitor's office opposite the Parish Church just a couple of minutes from the ground. A few days before Stock had walked across, popped his head round the door and said: 'Dick, I'm sorry to tell you but you're playing on Saturday.' Dyke, who was 6ft 2ins tall, a gentle man and a Sunday-school teacher, looked up and smiled. 'Jolly good', he said. He had played in only one first-team game – against Bath on Christmas Day.

The directors of the two clubs had a pre-match lunch at the Manor Hotel, a pleasant meal during which there were lengthy references to sportsmanship and lasting friendships. The Yeovil men did their best to sound optimistic but there was no doubting the confidence of Sunderland. It had been a long journey for them, and there was going to be little in the way of profit, but no one seriously suggested that Sunderland were likely to run into any other kind of problem.

Weak morning sunshine had given way to cloud when the two teams ran out on January 29th, 1949, with Yeovil sporting the Borough coat-of-arms on their new green shirts. Young Rex Rainey again led the way, and squeezed into place on the terraces were 17,100 people – the biggest crowd in Yeovil's history. The line-up: *Yeovil* – Dyke; Hickman, Davis;

Keeton, Blizzard, Collins; Hamilton, Stock, Bryant, Wright, Hargreaves. *Sunderland* – Mapson; Stelling, Ramsden; Watson, Hall, Wright; Duns, Robinson, Turnbull, Shackleton, Reynolds.

Yeovil started well and got better; they were more committed, more aggressive. Keeton, Blizzard and Collins were rock-firm in the middle of the field, Stock and Wright kept things moving briskly, and Hamilton quickly found he had the measure of both Sunderland full-backs. Hargreaves, on the other Yeovil wing, pulled a muscle early on but the Southern League side had already convinced themselves they were going to win.

The game was twenty-six minutes old when Yeovil went ahead and Stock, fittingly, was the scorer. A long free-kick and a clever flick of a head got the ball up to him – and, as Hall desperately tried to make contact, Stock swung and hit the ball sweetly with his left foot from the edge of the penalty area. 'I didn't have time to think about it', recalls Stock. 'I just hit the ball as hard as I could and in it went.' It was his first goal of the season and as he returned to the centre he reflected: 'I don't get many, but I get 'em at the right time.' He was conscious of the fact that the population of the town was less than 23,000 – and that 17,000 were at Huish.

Yeovil still led at half-time but right on the hour young Dyke made his first and only mistake of the match and Sunderland equalized. He jumped to save from Ramsden, fell over Turnbull and dropped the ball at the feet of Robinson who gratefully tapped it into an empty net. The game now was painfully tense. Yeovil became a little too eager and they were pulled up regularly for offside as Sunderland's defence began to get the hang of things and settle down.

After ninety minutes the score was still 1-1 and, to keep travelling costs down to a minimum in those days of economy, the game went straight into half-an-hour's extra-time. Yeovil began to spark once more, a side of fighters, and Sunderland's composure again started to fade.

In the primitive Press box, the nation's reporters could sense a major story in the making. They had no telephones, so copy was lowered to young colleagues at the rear. Among them was

David Foot, now a distinguished west country journalist, who recalls: 'I 'phoned my sports-editor's copy from a butcher's shop just across the road. This was after it had been deftly lowered by string from the lofty box to where I was positioned at the back of the stand – in the gents' urinals. I dictated with feverish excitement between the lamb-chops and still managed to see most of the match from a sneaky and privileged beer-crate perch by the side of Alec Stock's office. It was a beautiful match.'

The weather was now closing in. Fog was stealing over the ground and from the directors' box, a tall and rather weird wooden structure behind a corner flag, next to the dressing-rooms, it was becoming increasingly difficult to see what was going on at the far end of the pitch. The directors did not help themselves: they were all puffing away on cigars the size of rolling pins – an unaccustomed luxury for the Yeovil directors but in no phase of the game, they had decided, were they going to be outdone by Sunderland. The fog and the clouds of cigar smoke were an interesting combination.

Outside the ground there were hundreds who would have given their souls for any glimpse of the game. They were still living every second of it, however, because radios in the waiting police cars – volume full up – were relaying the BBC radio commentary of Raymond Glendenning.

Sunderland were playing a town as well as a team and it proved too much for them. Yeovil took the lead again with just a minute left of the first period of extra time. The scorer was Bryant and, living now in Dorset, he is still asked to describe his contribution to history. He tells it like this:

> Len Shackleton gave the ball away because he was dead scared of our right-half Bob Keeton. Bob pushed the ball through to Nick Collins and he moved it on to Ray Wright. A little push forward to me and I ran past their centre-half, got just inside the box and put the ball into the bottom left corner of the Sunderland net. I think what really won the match for us was the way Alec Stock wound us up before the match. He was such a marvellous talker he could have told us black was white and we would have believed him.

Now the minutes seemed to grow and multiply. Sunderland

drew again on their bruised pride and their attacks acquired shape and point. Yeovil, for their part, decided this was no time for all the finer things in the game. They were banging the ball forward as if they hated it, towards the Sunderland corner flags or, better still, up into the back row of the stand. They were tactics which hardly suited the First Division side and Shackleton, sidling up to Stock, said: 'Don't spoil a good game.' 'A good game!' retorted Stock, 'It's life and death.'

The fog and the tension got thicker together. Two leading referees, Jim Wiltshire, who had controlled the Cup Final a couple of years before, and Bill Edwards, were among the crowd and they decided they could not bear to watch any more. They went into Stock's office to suffer alone.

Three minutes from the end the referee, Mr W.F. Smith from Aldershot, blew his whistle for a Sunderland free-kick. The crowd thought it was the final whistle and surged triumphantly onto the pitch. Police and officials cleared them off with mounting desperation.

The free-kick was just outside the Yeovil penalty area and no one was in any doubt that the match was hanging on the slenderest of slender threads. There was now less than a minute left and Stock can still taste the tension:

> This was it. We lined up our defensive wall, four others and myself, and waited. 'Blokes', I said, 'if one of you duck you're bound to get the sack aren't you?' Barney Ramsden, Sunderland's left-back, came up to take the kick – a big fellow with thighs like tree-trunks. I had a vision of the ball carrying me into the back of the net. We braced ourselves but big Barney made a lovely mess of it, his foot seemed to hit the ground and as the ball bounced forward I think most of the Yeovil team made contact with it. There was no messing about. The ball went out of the ground and as far as I know it's still going. We'd done it.

The cheers of victory began thunderously and got louder. *Pulman's Weekly News* reported happily: 'The jubilant scenes were reminiscent of V.E. Day . . . it was Yeovil's day and as far as football was concerned it was the greatest day in history and the West country made the most of it . . . the town went wild with excitement and people who thronged the streets demonstrated their delight, forgetting their accustomed southern reserve.'

In the Yeovil boardroom, Colonel Joe Prior, Sunderland's chairman and a popular man noted for his grey-brown bowler and hunting crop, raised his glass to the Southern League club. 'It will be a shock back home', he said, 'but never in all my years in football have I experienced a warmer welcome than here at Yeovil.' Sunderland's manager Bill Murray was equally gracious in defeat: 'The pitch had nothing to do with the result. The simple truth is that we were beaten by a better side. We have no excuses. Yeovil played good Cup-tie football whereas Sunderland kept waiting for something that did not come.'

In their primitive wooden dressing-room, a place of steam and confusion, Yeovil's players answered the questions of the Press. Stan Abbott, his bald head glistening, moved around with his dirty old brown enamelled teapot. Alec Stock, that man of many parts, helped count the takings.

The *Sunderland Echo's* footballer reporter, writing under the pseudonym of 'Argus', saw the game at rather closer quarters than most of his colleagues. 'I reported this game from a school-desk on the field itself within inches of the touchline', he wrote. 'Occasionally a bugle sounded. Whether Sunderland thought it sounded the retreat I don't know.'

'Sunderland were humiliated', he added. 'Whatever Yeovil were against Sunderland they were not giant-killers, for there were no giants to kill. I have no intention of robbing gallant Yeovil of any of the sweets of victory. They earned them and deserved them. If Sunderland touched the depths that was their fault.'

It was left to the *Sunday People,* perhaps, to get nearest to the spirit abroad in Yeovil that Saturday night. It began its report the next morning: 'Hang out the flags! Ring the joybells! Let's go gay! Crown our team king of all! That was the sentiment in this football crazy Somerset town after Sunderland had been out-manoeuvred, out-paced and out-classed.'

Yeovil, the town and the team, discovered they were more than national news. Messages of congratulations, many from west country emigrants, arrived from Australia, South Africa and Canada, from Sweden, Switzerland and Germany. The

Mayor of Yeovil, Alderman B. Dening, was even rung up by the *Ontario Star*. 'People out here,' said a distant voice 'are thrilled by the way your little team beat the mighty Sunderland. There are many west country folk here and they want to know more about your team.' The interview lasted twenty-five minutes and cost £30.

Yeovil were in the fifth round for the first time in their lives and when they were drawn away to the holders of the Cup, Manchester United, the town could hardly believe it. The great city of Manchester . . . Matt Busby's United . . . in terms of distance and status it was a trip to the other side of the world. Yeovil immediately decided to make the most of it.

Six special trains took 3,000 supporters to Manchester and another 3,000 went by coach and car. Glove factories, works and businesses turned the occasion into their annual outing. The miles between Yeovil and Manchester seemed festooned with green and white.

Yeovil's team left home on Thursday morning and were seen off, to the accompaniment of engine whistles and factory hooters, by half the town. They nearly forgot a crate of eggs and sherry – which they had convinced themselves was an essential part of their training diet – and one or two of the players had to leap off the train at the last moment to pull it aboard. Every station they passed through was a blur of supporters, well-wishers and banners.

Matt Busby had already sent the club a message saying: 'A great welcome awaits you in Manchester.' He sensed the mood of his parish perfectly. The city opened its arms and hearts to the little team from Somerset: Alec Stock and his players found themselves fêted like heroes – back-slapped and hand-pumped on pavement and in shop by so many warm-hearted people that more than once the police had to be called.

Manchester United were then playing their League and Cup games at Maine Road, the home of Manchester City, because Old Trafford was still a war casualty. Maine Road was a big ground and on that early day in February 1949, it needed to be. Buses full of fans left Piccadilly in the heart of the city at the rate of one every thirty seconds and when the gates were closed twenty minutes before the kick-off there were 81,565 people inside and thousands more outside.

Yeovil made two changes from the side which beat Sunderland. Stan Hall was fit again and took over from Dickie Dyke in goal – Dyke, his fine display in the fourth round not forgotten, was soon to be offered professional terms at £3 a week – but Jackie Hargreaves was injured and Jack Roy, a busy, enterprising player, took his place on the wing.

United were a team of rich and beautifully harnessed ability. There were six full internationals in the side and they were 7-2 favourites to retain the Cup they had won so stylishly by beating Blackpool – Matthews, Mortensen and all – by four goals to two at Wembley the season before. Johnny Carey, a model captain and one of the great men of football, Allenby Chilton, Jack Rowley, Stan Pearson, Charlie Mitten, Jimmy Delaney . . . United's side bristled with talent of the choicest kind. They were, on paper and in reality, much too good for the Southern League part-timers.

Yeovil took the field to a cheer that nearly overwhelmed them and began the afternoon by winning a corner in the first thirty seconds. One of the largest crowds ever to have watched an FA Cup-tie, outside a final, sucked in its breath. Surely nothing was going to go wrong? But United soon pulled rank and for the rest of the game did much as they wanted. They scored eight, of which the powerful Rowley got five, and might well have doubled the score.

The details did not matter. It was a clean execution and the victims felt little pain. They had lived well and they died happily.

Manchester United reached the semi-finals of the Cup that season and finished runners-up to Portsmouth in the League. Yeovil won the Southern League Cup for the first time and, an equally singular achievement, they raised a smile on the face of their bank manager. Their Cup success earned them around £5,000.

Yeovil have been doing their level best ever since to join the League establishment: one day they will make it. But at Cup time every year their name is one to respect and one to avoid. Between 1925, when they played a League club for the first time, and 1981, the year of the 100th tournament, they reached the third round proper on nine occasions – a record unequalled by any other non-League club. Their reputation is matchless.

7 Norwich...1959

The Cup, unforgivably, got cold feet at 3.37 on the afternoon of Wednesday, March 18th, 1959. It chose that moment to slam the great gates of Wembley in the faces of some footballers from the heart of Norfolk's farming community, just as they were preparing to crown the finest giant-killing run of all by becoming the first Third Division side to reach the final.

It was the moment when Billy Bingham of Luton Town, an elf of an Irishman with a twinkle in his eyes and boots, scored the goal that beat Norwich City in a semi-final replay on the neutral grass of St Andrew's. It ended a ride on a magic carpet.

Norwich had beaten Ilford, Swindon and then four winners of the trophy, Manchester United, Cardiff, Tottenham and Sheffield United, before losing, undeservedly and narrowly, to another First Division side they had threatened to devour. Their eleven games were watched by nearly half a million people and their fame circled the globe. It was a fairy story which had everything except a happy ending; and afterwards, unashamedly, the Norwich players cried in their bath.

The team and their supporters redefined the meaning of 'Cup-fever'. They cared about victory and defeat as they cared about life and death. Their soul-stirring passion seemed to be about something more than sport. It was a swaggering demand for identity, a rebuke for a society that was too well-ordered, a nose thumbed at destiny. Norwich were centre stage for two glorious months and the nation loved them for their bravado. Their anthem, 'On the Ball, City', a noise that welled up from their innermost spirit, was one of the sounds of the fifties.

It was a march of triumph, which promised that one day a Third Division club will reach the final. Three Third Division clubs before them, Millwall in 1937, Port Vale in 1954 and York City in 1955, had reached the semi-finals; one more, Crystal Palace in 1976, has managed it since. Twice, of course, a Third Division club has won the League Cup at Wembley, Queen's

Park Rangers in 1967 and Swindon two years later, but the FA Cup has always been more mindful of standards. Perhaps, though, it now regrets the tawdry trick it played on Norwich on that spring day in 1959 and, who knows, it could merely be waiting for another club of their calibre to emerge from below stairs. We must be patient. The Third Division came into being in 1920 and a few more years will not hurt.

The city of Norwich itself, it needs to be said, does not immediately strike the visitor as a likely or proper place for fanaticism of any kind. There is a beautiful feeling of permanence about it: a city, this, of stout character, infinite charm and engaging curiosities, a city of handsome churches but not of piety or pompousness, a city of farming men, fighting men and men who know how to make and look after their money. It was alive and well long before football, and its heartbeat will still be strong when the game is only of interest to our social historians.

The town's football club, with a revealing sense of values, has been tucked round the back. You turn hard left outside the railway station, follow the bending waters of the Wensum for ten minutes and there is Carrow Road with its fresh complexion and straight-backed stands. It is part of the community but not, in a normal season, central to it. Season 1958-9 was not normal.

There had been earlier moments of high success in the Cup. As a Southern League club, already known as the Canaries because of their yellow and green colours and playing on a ground called the Nest along at Rosary Road, they made their first dent on the trophy by beating Liverpool at Anfield in 1909. Later, as one of the original members of the Third Division, they overcame Leeds in 1935, the year they moved to Carrow Road, Liverpool again in 1951 and, splendidly, Arsenal at Highbury in 1954. As a League club they made up the numbers and in 1957, with eight wins in forty-six games, they even had to apply for re-election; but in the Cup, as Sam Weller would have put it, they were 'werry fierce canaries'.

It was not until Archie Macauley took over as manager in the spring of 1957, however, that the club moved onto its front foot. Macauley, a wing-half of great distinction in his day but his red hair now greying at the temples, was the catalyst they needed.

Macauley inherited a club which had lost its pride. It was being kept alive, embarrassingly, by public subscription, the players wore shirts which were losing shape and thread, and their boots looked as if they were never cleaned from one match to the next. The fans were as dejected as the players, and Macauley once had to lock himself in his office to escape a posse of supporters bent on something much more basic than a chat about the next match.

Norwich's new man brought to the job all the style and wit he had shown as a player. Macauley had played for Glasgow Rangers, West Ham, Brentford, Arsenal (a member of their League championship side in 1947-8) and Fulham, and had been a right-half who was always cool, fluent and constructive. He was a beautiful ball-player who could also shoot with venom and bite hard in the tackle – good enough, in fact, to play for Scotland on seven occasions and for Great Britain against the Rest of Europe in 1947. He later joined Guildford City as player-manager and then Dundee, before moving to Norwich on the right-wing of England.

Macauley was a handsome man who could charm people as easily as he could a football, firm but fair, approachable and confiding but, as there must be in every manager, he had private and complex lines of thought. To some he might have seemed diffident. A manager walks alone and Macauley knew better than anyone the size of the job he had taken on. Norwich were short of patience as well as money.

He quickly assessed the players he had; some, he knew immediately, would do. There was Ron Ashman, who had signed for Norwich back in 1944, once a forward, then a wing-half but now a lean and flinty defender who was as much a part of the club as the stand and the pitch. Ken Nethercott, the goalkeeper, was another man who knew his job, a wry and popular westcountryman who had been with the club for ten years. Roy McCrohan, a solid and powerful influence at right-half, had been signed from Reading in 1951; Bobby Brennan, once of Distillery, Luton, Birmingham and Fulham, a Northern Ireland international and a winger of craft and great experience, joined them in 1953; Bryan Thurlow, Ashman's resolute full-back partner, had been on the pay-roll of the club since 1954; and Terry Bly, who was to be the goal-scoring hero of the Cup run, was a Norfolk lad who joined the club as an amateur and then signed professional forms in 1956.

Macauley had a half a team and he used a lot of words and energy plus a bit of money, mostly the income from advance season tickets, to complete his line-up. He paid a reasonable fee to Sheffield Wednesday for Barry Butler, a dreadnought of a centre-half, a fearless pillar of a man, and got Matt Crowe, his resourceful left-half, from Partick Thistle for £500. The following year, 1958, he added Terry Allcock, Errol Crossan and Jimmy Hill to the strength. Allcock was a busy maker and taker of chances at inside-right, a big Yorkshireman who was signed from Bolton; Crossan was a right-winger with enough speed to flummox most full-backs, a Canadian who had played for Manchester City, Gillingham and Southend; and Hill, soon to win the first of seven caps for Northern Ireland, was a compact and clever inside-left who had come from Newcastle.

It was a team of variety and balance, muscle and guile, promise and experience, a patchwork quilt of a side who enjoyed their football and also each other's company, a side shaped and glued together by the know-how of Macauley.

Ron Ashman, speaking more than two decades later as a manager himself, of Scunthorpe United, still remembers with admiration the contribution of Macauley:

> I played at Norwich for 21 years and of all the managers I was under there Archie was the best with tactics. He'd watch a team and then go through their strengths and weaknesses for us and say how they could be beaten – and nine and a half times out of ten he'd be right. We played wingers, Crossan had the speed, Brennan the craft, so sometimes Archie would say for example 'Their full-backs can't play . . . this is what we'll do.'
>
> We had tremendous faith in Archie. He'd been a real footballer himself – he could play a bit, that one – and he wanted all his teams to play football. He even wanted us to play football in defence, provided we didn't play too square and do silly things and get caught in possession. That was the way he always thought. We had to be positive.

Basically, we had a wing-half playing alongside the centre-half, say McCrohan back with Butler, and then an inside-forward – Hill or Allcock – linking up with Crowe in midfield. McCrohan was a long-striding player who could come forward quickly and the idea was to draw opponents on to us in the middle third of the field, then switch the ball out to the flanks, to our wingers, and in the middle, of course, we had Bly who could put them away and who always had plenty of support.

The first half of the 1958-9 season is not remembered in Norwich simply because there was nothing much to remember. Their victory over Reading at Carrow Road on Boxing Day was their first League win at home since late September. The side was desperately short of goals and Allcock was even dropped at one point; he was over-anxious, snatching at chances and the harder he tried the less he achieved. The one stroke of real luck they had was to be drawn at home to Ilford, a moderate Isthmian League side, in the first round proper. Norwich were then at their lowest ebb and, although they won by 3-1, they had more than their fair share of fortune.

By the time the second round arrived, though, Norwich were picking up: a 1-1 draw at Swindon, a sparkling 1-0 victory in the replay. The prize was a home tie against Manchester United and now, suddenly, the mood began to change. Backs straightened with pride in the town's ale-houses and news of the team on the back pages was read and reread before such routine matters as insurrections and disasters were turned to on the front. The local police began to wonder what problems five thousand United fans and a full house at Carrow Road might cause.

Norwich's players, to their surprise and then delight, discovered that everything they did and nearly did became fodder for the media machine. It was even revealed that three players, Ashman, Crowe and Crossan, had given up smoking and that three more, Nethercott, Bly and Brennan, had cut their intake down to one cigarette a day. 'The players', Macauley was reported as saying, 'did it all by themselves.'

Manchester United were still rebuilding after the Munich disaster of the previous February, but they had reached the Cup

Finals of 1957 and 1958, and their victory over Blackpool the week before their third-round visit to Carrow Road was their eighth in a row. The bookmakers saw United as 19-2 second favourites for the Cup. Norwich, at 2,000-1, were hardly seen at all.

Carrow Road had already had a look at Bobby Charlton that season. He had scored two of the three goals by which England beat Czechoslovakia in an Under-23 international there, and the crowd had relished his surging pace and murderous shooting. Norwich, however, did their own homework. They watched United play three times and Macauley found himself with a folder of notes. 'This information covers ten members of United's side – the odd man out is Bobby Charlton', said the Norwich manager with only a flicker of a smile. 'It's no use telling my lads what to do against Bobby because I don't know what to expect myself. He is probably the finest match-winner in football today. We are just keeping our fingers crossed that he's not in the mood.'

Privately, Macauley spent much of his time building up his own players' confidence. The week before they had beaten Southend by four goals to nil, with Bly and Crossan each scoring in the first ninety seconds of the match. The team had looked in marvellous shape, with skill flourishing inside a framework of sweat and discipline, and Macauley insisted that nothing was beyond them. He recalled that Arsenal had been beaten by Bradford in his own days at Highbury. The Norwich players began to believe something might be on.

United, for their part, were feeling pretty sure of themselves: they were undefeated since mid-November and their football, once again, was a delight to watch. Albert Quixall, the young but celebrated England inside-forward for whom United paid Sheffield Wednesday a record £45,000, had found his golden touch at last. He had taken a couple of months to settle down but now he was combining well with Charlton. The blond Quixall was full of light and shade, a player of wit and style, while Charlton's abundant qualities seemed to have acquired a brand-new sheen.

Warren Bradley, on the right-wing, was another player United had brought in to repair the damage of Munich. He was a former amateur international with Bishop Auckland but made such progress that within a year he won full England caps against Italy, Mexico and the United States. Dennis Viollet, a sensitive player and a slick, lethal finisher, had moved to centre-forward and was obviously relishing the role.

Behind them were yeomen of the quality of Harry Gregg, Northern Ireland's goalkeeper and a man of whom Charlton was to say 'just seeing Harry between the posts gave me confidence' and Billy Foulkes, a large and dedicated defender who was to play for the club on more than 600 occasions – two men who, like Charlton, Viollet and left-winger Albert Scanlon, had survived the horror of the air crash.

On the morning of the game United's fans poured into Norwich like a conquering army. The city was soon awash with their colourful dress and language. They generated so much heat that they hardly noticed the wretched weather and spared no thought for a Carrow Road pitch which by now was covered with a thin blanket of snow and ice.

United's players knew the moment they stepped onto the field, though, that winter had lined up with Norwich. The teams – *Norwich:* Nethercott; Thurlow, Ashman; McCrohan, Butler, Crowe; Crossan, Allcock, Bly, Hill, Brennan. *Manchester United:* Gregg; Foulkes, Carolan; Goodwin, Cope, McGuiness; Bradley, Quixall, Viollet, Charlton, Scanlon.

The issue was never in doubt. Norwich were blunt and uncomplicated; they were not frightened by United or inhibited by the conditions. Bly, just twenty-two-years old and playing in his second Cup-tie, was a holy terror, Allcock had moments of devastating inspiration, Crossan mastered Carolan, McCrohan and Crowe were a swift, sure link between attack and defence, Butler was a rock, and Thurlow, after a nervous start, and Ashman looked unbeatable. Nethercott made only a modest contribution, but that was not his fault. United managed just one shot of quality, from Scanlon, which the Norwich goalkeeper saved brilliantly, and afterwards Nethercott had to admit: 'I've never had an easier afternoon in my life.'

United clearly did not relish the conditions or Norwich's ravenous appetite for battle. Charlton and Quixall were dragons without teeth and the players around them made so many elementary errors that the crowd of 38,000 must have wondered if they were witnessing a massive conspiracy.

Gregg was the only United player to walk off the field with any credit. The athletic Irish goalkeeper made five breathtaking saves and was the difference to his side between mere embarrassment and disgrace. As it was Norwich won by three goals to nil, with Bly scoring twice, his second near the end a fine solo effort, and Crossan heading in another.

The stands and terraces of Carrow Road had taken a little while to believe the evidence of their own eyes, but once they grasped what was happening the thunder of their support physically widened the gap between the two sides. They were not mere onlookers; they were part of the conflict. From that day on, Norwich's opponents were to be faced by a team of tens of thousands.

The United fans, who had filled this corner of Norfolk with their boasts and obscenities in the morning, were now sullen and silent. There was at least one man, however, who knew how to lose with dignity. Ten minutes after the end the green door of the Norwich dressing-room opened and Matt Busby walked in. 'Congratulations', he said. 'You were the better side and you won on merit.'

Norwich discovered it could celebrate with the best. Its folk rewrote most of the manuals on eating, boozing, whoopee-making and party-giving. Practice even improved them and stories of that night and others which followed that season are still told with reverence.

The draw for the fourth round gave Norwich another home tie, this time against Cardiff, a better than average Second Division club, who had beaten Plymouth Argyle by 3-0 on their own ground in the previous round. All tickets for the game somehow disappeared in a matter of hours and Cardiff, equally confident of a healthy Cup run, sent up three special trains full of supporters.

Cardiff proved to be tougher all round, physically and mentally, than Manchester United and although Norwich won by 3-2 it is a game remembered by Ron Ashman with a special mixture of pride and relief. 'It was the hardest game we had: we all thought that', he recalls. 'They really made us go. We were down to them early on and only got the winner right at the end. They matched us in all the things we thought were our strengths and if they had taken us to a replay at their ground I don't think many of us would have fancied our chances.'

The early part of the game was Cardiff's property. They took the lead through Ron Hewitt after sixteen minutes and then, playing as if they were going to canter to victory, they missed three comfortable chances. The Welsh fans were singing 'Land of my Fathers' . . . the Norwich crowd were quiet. City were clearly not on the ball.

Three minutes into the second half, however, Crossan knocked in an equalizer and seven minutes later – the stands and terraces now coming alive – Allcock nodded down a long free-kick from Ashman, and Bly, first to think, first to move, put Norwich in front. Tempers became frayed, both teams were warned to cool down and when Allcock had to leave the field for treatment Cardiff exploited the situation in a twinkling. Joe Bonson made it 2-2 with nineteen minutes left. The groundwork had been done for the grand climax.

There were just three minutes and forty seconds left on the stopwatch held by Cardiff's manager Bill Jones, when his captain and left-back Ron Stitfall tried to place a clearance instead of clouting it into the Norfolk Broads. 'Don't ask me why', said Stitfall afterwards. Crossan hopefully stuck out a leg and succeeded in toe-ending the ball to Bly – and Bly, that natural predator, reacted instinctively. 'I didn't have time and I couldn't see a gap', he admitted, 'so I just smashed the ball and hoped.' It squeezed between Cardiff's goalkeeper Ron Nicholls and the near post. Norwich 3, Cardiff 2 . . . and it was party-time again.

Next came Tottenham Hotspur at White Hart Lane, a club, a stage and a challenge that reduced – or elevated – the city of Norwich to an authentic case of mass hysteria. It would doubtless have been worse if they had known that in another eighteen months or so Spurs were going to become the first club of this century to complete the League and Cup double.

Every angle was handsomely exploited. There was, for example, an old relationship between Bly and Tottenham's centre-half Maurice Norman who had been sold by Norwich to Spurs: they had played together in the Norwich 'B' team. Now, though, they faced each other in a top-of-the-bill heavyweight bout . . . and the introductions went something like this. 'In the yellow and green corner, standing 6ft and weighing in at 12st 3lbs, the goal-scoring sensation of the season, the ex-plumber from Fincham (population 619) – Terry Bly. And in the white and blue corner, at 6ft 1in and 12st 11lb, Mr Granite himself, the ex-farmer's boy from Mulbarton (pop. 469) – Maurice Norman.' It was all good stuff.

The Norwich bandwagon was rolling along at a brisk pace. They were attracting money and the bookmakers prudently cut their odds to win the Cup, first to 250-1, next to 200-1 and then to a straight hundred. Spurs were holding steady at 10-1.

Another kind of investor appeared on the scene, someone new to Norwich. The spiv wanted his slice of the action. There were big touts and little opportunists everywhere asking £1 for 2s 6d ground tickets and £8 for a ten-bob stand seat. There were even cunning local folk who motored down to London, queued for tickets at White Hart Lane and then returned to make a killing. They were taking a risk because the Norwich fans soon worked out their own little answer to the problem. They would 'talk' to a spiv, take his tickets, pay him their face value – and, if the river happened to be handy, they would then throw him in.

Macauley again named an unchanged Norwich side, but Tottenham's manager Bill Nicholson had a problem. Danny Blanchflower, the current Footballer of the Year, was in the reserves and not enjoying a moment of it. This immensely gifted and articulate Irish international had been through a lean spell but he considered he was through it and was pressing for his place in the first team. He had asked for a transfer which was firmly refused on his 33rd birthday – no move and no place for him, either, in the side to face Norwich. Nicholson decided to keep an unchanged team.

The city of Norwich woke early on the morning of February 14th, 1959. More than 20,000 were going to the match and the first of them left soon after five o'clock. The rest followed in fourteen special trains, six scheduled trains and every coach, hire-car and taxi (at £10 and more a head) in the area. The staff at Norwich station admitted they were 'bewildered' and shopkeepers in the city resigned themselves to a miserable day's business. The Norwich fans even took North London by surprise: White Hart Lane was turned into a corner of Norfolk. The gates were closed with 67,633 people inside, and the East Anglians out-roared, out-sung, out-rattled and out-glittered their rivals.

They saw a fine and enthralling match but not a clear-cut result. Spurs started confidently but their Third Division opponents, once they had settled down, proved to be the more aggressive, more adaptable side and when Allcock gave them the lead in the 64th minute it promised to be enough to send them into the quarter-finals.

Cliff Jones, Spurs Welsh international left-winger, a mercurial threat to every defence of his time, confesses he thought the game was over:

> We were not playing well and on the day Norwich should have won with a bit to spare. Luck seemed to be on our side, though and the biggest bit came in the very last minute.
>
> Tommy Harmer took a corner, Dave Dunmore helped it on and Jim Iley tried a shot, but he sliced it so badly that the ball went back to Dunmore. 'What a pass!' Jim kept saying afterwards. By this time I had moved across to the inside-position, and although I realized as the ball came across again that Bobby Smith and Maurice Norman were probably better positioned I thought 'This is our last chance – take it.' The ball skipped through at a nice height and I hit it on the volley with my left foot. I saw Ron Ashman try to push the ball over the bar with his hand but it went in just inside the left post.
>
> We were OK for a replay but I had a price to pay. Bryan Thurlow had obviously been ordered to play me out of the game and he did his job very well. He spent the afternoon thumping into me and I didn't enjoy it much. As we left the field Thurlow came up to me and said, 'Sorry Cliff, but this is the Cup.' I remember thinking to myself, 'That's why you're so bloody good at it.'

Nicholson was suddenly not so sure the team he had picked was the best one, and he announced immediately that there would be changes for the replay. He dropped Dunmore, the pint-sized Harmer and Johnny Brooks, and brought in Blanchflower, Terry Medwin and Eddie Clayton. They lined up like this: Hollowbread; Baker, Hopkins; Dodge, Norman, Iley; Medwin, Blanchflower, Smith, Clayton, Jones. Norwich were again unchanged.

The match was unforgettable: a fierce and taut battle which involved every player, fan and blade of grass inside Carrow Road. Norwich were again a force of nature but Spurs, this time, showed committment to match their skill. Blanchflower was a major influence, cool and steadying, Mel Hopkins and Peter Baker, their full-backs, took on Crossan and Brennan with intelligence and weight, and Bobby Smith was a muscular trouble-maker in front. Norwich had their bad moments and Nethercott was forced to make four brilliant saves, each one it seemed better than the last, but not once did any man lower his head.

There was no score at half-time and Norwich, primed and lifted by Macauley, began the second-half like a force-ten gale. They kept it up, too, and in the 63rd minute Bly confirmed his status as a national hero. Ashman lifted another of his long, hard-driven passes into the Spurs penalty area where the ball bounced off a Spurs' limb and ran to Bly. The tall Norwich centre-forward simply drifted past Norman before placing his shot wide of John Hollowbread in the Spurs goal. It was a masterly piece of finishing – quick, clinical, devastating.

Every minute from that point on seemed to contain 120 seconds. Geoffrey Watling, Norwich's chairman, a straight and expensively suited man, was sitting next to Macauley and he began to count off the minutes. 'Ten . . . nine . . . eight . . . seven . . . ' Macauley decided he could take no more. 'Mr Chairman', he roared above the clamour, 'Will you shut up!'

The Norwich team and their fans were now in perfect harmony, one feeding hungrily off the other. Ashman remembers: 'The crowd was so tremendous that in all my time in football I never experienced anything else like it. The atmosphere was absolutely electric. It seemed to cut the air. It made your hair tingle. We were on a sort of "high". There was simply no way we could lose – and we all knew it.' They were right, of course. Norwich 1, Spurs 0. The city reached for its bottle-openers.

John Bromley, writing in the *Daily Herald*, captured the mood of it all: 'Mac's Marvels march on! All hell broke loose at Norwich last night when the golden boot of Terry Bly flattened Spurs . . . and kicked London right out of the Cup. Picture that winning goal. People stood on their stand seats waving their arms and Bly did a victory leap before being swallowed up in a mob of yellow shirts.' Such reports were read a dozen times the following morning before being carefuly pasted into scrap-books. Norwich, they felt in heart and bone, were going to win the Cup and every step along the road to Wembley was something to cherish.

The draw for the quarter-finals on the following Monday might have dampened the fervour in lesser towns: Norwich were drawn away to Sheffield United who, in style and consistency, were one of the best teams in Division Two. They were a mixture of ambition and steel and, in fact, were to finish the season in third place above clubs of the calibre of Liverpool, Stoke and Derby County. The Norwich fans, however, merely looked forward to another good outing and another good win.

There were 35,000 applications for 14,000 tickets for the game at Bramall Lane. Supporting City had become a way of life. Women varnished their finger-nails alternately in yellow and green; hours of hard work went into making canary costumes; baby dolls in ancient prams were dressed and decorated in the club's colours. Thousands of fans spent every free hour just hanging around the ground. The club's telephone number was engaged by the hour.

Macauley's son went down with 'flu and, taking no chances, the Norwich manager kept away from his players for a day or two. He also had passing fitness doubts about Allcock and Thurlow, but on the day before his club's first-ever quarter-final he was again able to name an unchanged side. Sheffield United fielded the side which had beaten Arsenal in the previous round and conceded only seven goals in their fourteen League games at home: Hodgkinson; Coldwell, Graham Shaw; Hoyland, Joe Shaw, Summers; Lewis, Hamilton, Pace, Russell, Simpson.

United knew the size of their task only too well. They had trained like commandoes and began the game as if they were bent on taking a vital beach-head. Their pace was furious, Norwich seemed a little bemused and Bill Russell gave the Sheffield club the lead. The goal, however, seemed to do Norwich more good than United. They stepped up their own pace, became more assertive and began to play better football; this was more like it.

Right on the hour, though, Norwich had one of the rare bits of bad luck in their Cup run. Ken Nethercott dislocated a shoulder and – a goal down, away from home and minus a proper goalkeeper – their prospects of turning the game inside-out in the last half hour looked on the dark side of black.

Ashman recalls that Macauley wanted Nethercott off the field with Brennan dropping back into goal. 'But we said we'd protect Ken – it was as daft as that. Barry Butler shouted 'Let him stay on' or choice words to that effect. It was just a feeling we had. We knew we wouldn't have stood much of a chance with only ten men, so I told Ken to keep going and said we'd look after him. As it happened he didn't have much to do but he got along by using his body and his one good arm.'

It was a gamble that was part folly, part heroism, but it came off. Crossan got an equalizer in the 73rd minute after a brilliant dribble by Brennan, and the score remained 1-1 even though Macauley admits he 'died a thousand deaths' in the last ten minutes. Yorkshiremen may be a tough, uncompromising breed, men who live to win, but they are the first to recognize and respect courage, and at the end the Bramall Lane regulars raised their red and white favours in a spontaneous salute to the Norwich players.

Another replay, another sell-out; for the fourth time 38,000 paid £6,000 for the privilege of sharing in the Odyssey. The Sheffield club's share of the tickets was 9,000 but, by hook and crook, Norwich fans got their hands on at least three-quarters of that allocation. It required time, patience, deviousness and money . . . in short, no problem or sacrifice at all.

The traffic in Norwich on the evening of the replay suggested the crowd was going to be in the region of 100,000. The Automobile Association reported that on one major road vehicles were entering the city at the rate of 200 an hour at 4 p.m., 600 at 5 p.m., 700 to 800 to 5 p.m. and, soon afterwards, 1,000. On another road, where there was only a single lane because of roadworks, the police simply turned off the traffic lights and let everything roar through in the direction of Carrow Road. Nothing was going the other way. Seven buses were involved in a totally motionless jam at the corner of Rosary Road.

Nethercott's injury meant Norwich had to make the first change of their Cup run. His place in goal was taken by Sandy Kennon, a powerful 6ft 2in South African who had been with Huddersfield for three years and had just joined the Norfolk club for a trial. His experience was limited, but he was large and confident and determined to make good use of his chance.

Sheffield United must have felt they did not have a friend in the world as they took the field. They played their part in a Cup-tie of suffocating tension, relentless pace and five goals; but it was a game they were never going to win. The army of photographers there knew it, too, and almost to a man they clustered and crouched behind the Sheffield goal.

Norwich took the lead after only thirteen minutes when United's England goalkeeper Alan Hodgkinson gave the ball away with a sloppy clearance and Crossan, equal to the opportunity, crossed from the left edge of the Sheffield penalty area. The ball reached Brennan awkwardly but he neatly adjusted his balance, switched the ball from his right foot to his left and from sixteen yards shot cleanly into a top corner of the net. No one in Norfolk could have misunderstood the roar that signalled that moment – and from the terraces one small boy ran onto the field and embraced Crossan.

The rest of Carrow Road waited. They sensed their time was coming, a feeling that hardened into conviction after half an hour when Bly ran smoothly onto a pass from the aggressive Allcock to put Norwich two ahead. A crowd of children ran onto the pitch this time, but still the rest waited. Derek Pace, a former Aston Villa man, pulled one back for United seven minutes later and now the battle was properly joined. The crowd's support was physical; it approached hysteria. McCrohan and Crowe were in magnificent form and the defence – with Butler looking taller and broader by the minute – soaked up punishment unflinchingly.

No one was in any doubt that the next goal was going to be the crucial one . . . and it was scored for Norwich by Bly – who else! – twenty minutes from the end. It was not the best goal of the night, or even the last one, because Gerry Summers got another for United, but it proved to be the winner. United fought like devils for the equalizer but Norwich, heroically, held on.

Norwich 3, Sheffield United 2 – and Alan Clarke, commentating for BBC Radio, saw the finish like this:

> There's the whistle for time, and what a scene as you can well imagine. Children, children, children everywhere, flooding the pitch. And policemen, too, trying to get the players off the pitch. Well, it's been a great performance! What a night for Norwich! Oh boy, oh boy . . . I'm going to stay here tonight. It should be a great night in the town. A great effort, they fought all the way with good skill and they took their chances. Luton (in the semi-final) will have to watch out for this Cup-fighting Norwich because it's right in their blood at this moment and you could never believe by this performance tonight that they are, in fact, in the Third Division.

Clarke's words that night were relished all over Norfolk and, Yorkshire excluded perhaps, enjoyed by the whole country. At the Lido ballroom the City's Lord Mayor, Councillor N.R. Tillett, rose to his feet as soon as he heard the result, raised his glass to 350 guests and said simply: 'Ladies and Gentlemen, the toast is . . . ON TO WEMBLEY.' At another dinner, speakers were allowed to get to their feet only if they promised to keep things short. Guests were more interested in listening to the commentary. Hotels, bars and off-licences were overrun. The City literally ran out of champagne.

The *Eastern Daily Press* summed things up with gusto the next morning:

> A great match, a great Cup-tie – from any point of view. Twice City went into a two-goal lead, twice Sheffield fought and schemed their way back to striking distance, and for the last seven minutes – which seemed like seven hours of a long

night watch – Norwich had to withstand a terrific onslaught. Yet in the end they were still looking for the opening, and almost in the last breath Crossan bounced a shot onto the wrong side of the bar.

As the seconds ticked by after United's second goal, which came in the 83rd minute, the seething fire in the thousands upon thousands of hearts which packed the terraces was bubbling and roaring and hardly able to contain itself. Such was the atmosphere that it might have been Cardiff Arms Park with Wales in sight of a Rugby Union victory over the English. After hearing the fervour and emotion that went into the echoing choruses of 'On the Ball, City' one is tempted to comment that 'we understand they can also sing in Wales'.

Now only Luton Town stood between Norwich and the epic distinction of becoming the first Third Division club to play in an FA Cup Final. No one in the City contemplated failure, and even if a doubting thought had occurred to anyone it would have been stifled at birth. Treason has always been a capital offence.

The Norwich faithful looked at Luton and were not over-impressed. They were a First Division club, true, and on the way to the semi-finals they had beaten Leeds by 5-1, Leicester by 4-1 in a replay, Ipswich by 5-2 and Blackpool by 1-0 in another replay. The Bedfordshire club also had a healthy leavening of internationals in their side. Syd Owen, their captain and centre-half, was thirty-six but he was an England international, lean and fit and wonderfully consistent; Allan Brown, at inside-right, was a Scottish cap and a telling blend of craft and experience; Ron Baynham, another England international, was rated by many as the best goal keeper in the country; Billy Bingham had been a regular member of Northern Ireland's side for seven years, a fast and highly elusive right-winger who had scored five vital Cup goals that season; and George Cummins, their inside-right, was a Republic of Ireland international and in his day an effective and clever ball-player.

All this was appreciated by the Norwich fans but – with transcending faith – they still saw Luton as just another stepping-stone along the road to Wembley. Twenty-two thousand of them travelled to White Hart Lane for the semi-final, happily convinced that by evening they would be looking forward to six weeks of fun and games before the final on the first Saturday of May. Norwich were unchanged, with Kennon still in goal, while Luton lined up like this: Baynham; McNally, Hawkes; Groves, Owen, Pacey; Bingham, Brown, Morton, Cummins and Gregory.

Norwich, it soon became apparent, were not at their best. They were not playing badly but they lacked their usual sureness of touch, they were making too many mistakes, and few were surprised when Luton took the lead after half an hour with a headed goal by Brown. Norwich kept on challenging and chasing, though, and in the 65th minute their industry was rewarded. Norwich attacked along the right-wing, John Groves tackled Hill and the Third Division club got a throw-in which put McCrohan in possession. He centred and, as half a dozen heads stretched upwards, the ball ran to Brennan who marked his 34th birthday by putting the ball past Baynham's right hand into a corner of the net.

There were some scares to come, Kennon again justifying his selection by making two fine saves, and one moment of desperation, Crowe bringing down Bingham with a passable imitation of a Rugby tackle, but Norwich proved once more that they could absorb punishment as well as give it. They earned the right to fight again.

The Norwich fans immediately saw the score line as a good omen. In three of the previous rounds, against Swindon, Spurs and Sheffield United, a 1-1 draw had been followed by victory in the replay. They were convinced their team could outlast anyone. They also relished the fact that in the other semi-final Nottingham Forest had beaten Aston Villa at Hillsborough at the first time of asking. Norwich were now in the last three of the Cup!

The replay was to be staged at St Andrew's, the home of Birmingham City, the following Wednesday afternoon, and Norwich spent the night before tucked away in a picturesque half-timbered hotel at Stratford-on-Avon. Paul Robeson, playing Othello at the Memorial Theatre, was a fellow guest. The atmosphere was relaxed, the mood confident; if there was tension it did not show.

The two teams were unchanged but the balance of the game was very different. Norwich were back on song, applying pressure, cutting sharply into their tackles, chasing every ball and cause, using the full width of the pitch and getting men into the Luton penalty area. They were not pretty to watch, but they looked too much of a handful for a Luton side whose game seemed curiously low-key for a match of such obvious importance. Luton's attack, in turn, made little impression on a Norwich defence that, once again, was ruggedly stable.

A Norwich victory looked a very good bet, but there is a higher destiny which decides on the names of the two clubs to play at Wembley; and Luton were the chosen ones.

Twelve minutes into the second half . . . and Alan Clarke takes up commentary again: 'Free-kick to Luton, in the inside-left position in the Luton half, pretty well half-way inside their half. Being placed by Gregory who's moving with his back to us. He'll take it, I think, with his right foot – and it's a good drive there – a header out by Norwich, out to the far side – but Allan Brown's racing for it on the edge – trying to round the full-back, skipper Ashman – and does so – turns the ball inside – Morton a back-heeler – a first time shot by Bingham . . . and it's there.' Luton 1, Norwich 0.

Norwich did not give in, of course, and on another day they might have scored three or four. But this time even Bly's shots were going wide of their mark, sometimes only by inches, and Luton had two men at the heart of their defence who were outstanding, goalkeeper Baynham and above all Owen, who kept a tight rein on everyone around him, colleagues as well as opponents.

Brendan McNally, Luton's right-back, finally stopped a shot on the line and that, symbolically, seemed to settle the issue. A few minutes later the whistle confirmed it. Norwich's famous Cup run had ended in the shadow of Wembley. The flight of the Canaries was over.

Syd Owen, who was soon to be named as the Footballer of the Year and then to become Luton's manager, said afterwards: 'I was hoping and praying Norwich didn't get an equalizer – I didn't fancy extra-time. After we'd scored Norwich tended to get a bit desperate which somehow, despite all the pressure they put on us, helped us consolidate and keep compact. Norwich are all about endeavour and spirit, but they're also skilful and constructive and I cannot understand why they're down in the Third Division.'

Ron Ashman still remembers the misery of the Norwich dressing-room. 'I've never seen so many grown men crying or near to crying. There were even tears in the bath. It hurt so much because we felt that Luton were there for the taking. They'd given us less trouble than almost anyone. We'd come all that way just to be beaten like that.'

It was Luton's night, but it was not to be their Cup. They were beaten 2-1 by Nottingham Forest in the final, despite Forest having to play with ten men for nearly an hour. Perhaps, though, Forest knew it was going to be their year. In the third round they had been drawn away to Tooting and Mitcham, an enterprising amateur side from the Isthmian League, and at half-time they were two goals down on a frozen pitch full of ridges and pot-holes. Only a side destined to win the Cup could have got out of that mess . . . and Forest did, with the help of an own goal and a fiercely disputed penalty.

Archie Macauley's Norwich were beaten in the first round by Reading the following season but balanced the books by winning promotion. Soon the side broke up and scattered. Butler, that wonderful defender, was killed in a car crash. Some, like Ashman, stayed in football. One became a draughtsman, another a salesman and others tried their luck in distant corners of the world. But they had got the club rolling. Norwich won the League Cup in 1962 and reached the final again, this time at Wembley, in 1973 and 1975. There was even one heady week early in season 1979-80 when they hit the top of the First Division.

The joy of that Cup run in 1959 can be seen now as part of their growing-up process. They will never know such moments again.

8 Oxford... 1964

Mr Justice Lawton may not have known much about football but he knew about people. He announced on the afternoon of Friday, February 14th, 1964, that Oxford Assizes would not, as planned, be sitting the following afternoon. 'I understand', he said, 'that for many people their loyalty to a certain activity of the City will conflict with their duty to the court.'

The chances are that had the learned judge decided to sit that Saturday afternoon he would have had the court to himself and given new weight to Mr Bumble's claim that 'the law is a ass'.

The 'certain activity' not identified by Mr Justice Lawton was Oxford United's fifth-round Cup-tie against Blackburn Rovers at the Manor Ground. It was, from every angle and by any yardstick, an unusual match: it was the first time that a member of the six-year-old Fourth Division had reached this stage of the tournament, it was watched by Oxford's first assembly of more than 20,000, and it attracted wider publicity than any sporting event in the City since Roger Bannister ran the first mile in under four minutes there in 1954.

Above all, though, the match was remarkable because Oxford United won it by three goals to one. It was a classic example of the Cup's ability to confound the inevitable: the distance between the two clubs in the game's pecking order had looked as wide and as deep as the Atlantic and Pacific rolled together.

Blackburn were one of the League's original twelve clubs, twice League champions, winners of the Cup three years in succession between 1884-6 and on six occasions altogether. The club's 1964 side was considered their best since the Second World War, and that season they had beaten Spurs 7-2 on their own Ewood Park, Wolves 5-1 at Molineux and West Ham at Upton Park 8-2. They were second in the First Division, second favourites for the Cup and considered by many sane and reputable judges to be a good bet for the 'Double'. Their side bristled with internationals.

Oxford United had somewhat less to boast about. Only a couple of years before they had been playing in the Southern League as Headington United, a club of dreamers a decent bus ride to the east of the city. They even had an identity problem: there was another, more central club in the parish, Oxford City, an amateur club with a professional ring to its name and more than one visitor found himself directed to the wrong ground. But in the early sixties Headington United began to grow, with all the inevitable physical and emotional problems of adolescence. They changed their name to Oxford United, which meant the rest of the world knew at last where they were, and on June 2nd, 1962, beneath the chandeliers of the Cafe Royal, they were voted into the League. As Southern League champions they took the place of poor Accrington Stanley. They finished eighteenth in their first season in the Fourth Division, and it was in the course of their equally modest second season that they astonished themselves, Blackburn and the world of football. It gave Oxford United their place in history as the first Fourth Division club to reach the quarter-finals.

It was the high-water mark of a Cup run which had a profound influence on sport in Oxford, a city which had been one of the cradles and then the fortress of amateurism. Sport in Oxford had always been given its spirit and direction by the university; it fostered an attitude of mind, free, expressive, romantic. The university had helped launch the FA Cup nearly a century before, stiffened England's cricket sides with initials and quality, and championed the game of Rugby Union all over the Empire. Its young men gathered their memories at the Parks and Iffley Road, and at the heart of its footballing traditions were names like the legendary Corinthians, Tommy Thompson's Pegasus and the Centaurs.

Now, though, United gave professional sport a place of its own in the city's affections; their achievements were admired in hall and quadrangle as well as office and factory floor. But at the same time United's progress innocently reflected more sinister trends in Oxford. Since the Second World War, industry had been superimposing itself on the city and university. Old Oxford endured, mellow and timeless, but now it was surrounded by much of the worst of the twentieth century. New roads cut their way through history, and factories mushroomed. The motorcar took the place of the bike. The 'Home of Lost Causes' was also the 'Home of Pressed Steel'. Judgement Day, for some planners and money-makers, will be an uncomfortable business.

United, however, were untroubled by such thoughts. They were not responsible in any way for the erosion of Oxford and, in any case, their progress in the Cup filled their days with mounting hope and ambition. Luck was obviously with them. They were given two non-League clubs to start them off and happily found themselves drawn at home in each of the six rounds in which they competed. The story unfolded in its own time but there was always a feeling about it inside the cramped and modest confines of the Manor. Their confidence, once they had beaten Blackburn and reached the quarter-finals, was nicely captured by the local boast: 'Two steps to Wembley . . . three to Europe.' They meant it, too. The Cup is full of opium.

Even Arthur Turner, Oxford United's manager, caught the mood, and with thirty-three years in the game he was old enough and wise enough to have known better. 'This must be my year', he was heard to muse early in the run . . . later he was saying 'This is my year.' But there was no doubting the part played by this ample extrovert in United's promotion from the ranks and in their remarkable Cup run.

Turner was a man of football. He had been a sterling centre-half with Stoke from 1931 to 1939, played for Birmingham just before and after the war and then rounded off his playing career with a couple of seasons at Southport. He cut his managerial teeth with Crewe, spent two seasons as Stoke's assistant-manager and then returned to another of his old clubs, Birmingham, and soon guided them back into Division One. Turner resigned in 1958, swearing he would never manage another League club, and took over Headington United early in 1959 – a nice, uncomplicated post with a club that everyone in the game knew was heading nowhere very fast.

That, at least, was the way it seemed; the truth was somewhat different. Headington proved to be a club ripe for bigger things and waiting patiently for a catalyst. Turner might have been sent by Heaven. He was an astute publicist who knew how to sell a club and he had the contacts, particularly in the Midlands, to pick up the right kind of players at the right price. He was a strong-featured man, larger than life, not always very tactful but – when the mood took him – excellent company. He liked a good chat and, if anyone had some worthwhile advice, he was a willing listener. He loved his football and never counted the hours when he was working. His experience had been gained in all four divisions of the League and, under his clever stewardship, Oxford grew wings.

Turner had a fine rapport, above all, with Ron Atkinson, his captain and right-half and the main pillar and inspiration of the side. Atkinson, later to become the accomplished manager of Cambridge United, West Bromwich Albion, and Manchester United, was responsible for much of the team's tactical thinking and, in this respect, there were times when his words seemed to count for more than Turner's. But the Oxford manager did not mind; he had a great respect for Atkinson and listened to him carefully.

Atkinson was only twenty-four at the time, a powerful Liverpudlian, 6ft tall and 13 stone, who was affectionately known as 'The Tank'. He was one of Turner's first signings, and the best. He had played for Birmingham's Youth side and then joined Aston Villa, but his future there as an inside-forward seemed limited and Turner, an excellent judge of ability and character, got him on a free transfer. Turner switched him to wing-half and soon made him his captain – and Atkinson, an open, humorous man, became one of the key figures in Oxford's success story. He was a vital influence, strong, stable and keen to take hold of a game. He could have bad games – and when he did there were no half measures; they were real stinkers – but on song or not he usually found a way to help the players around him and make them play above themselves.

The Oxford side was an interesting company. There were weaknesses and deficiencies in the structure but there was also experience, muscle, talent of various shapes and shades and, lacing them together, a corporate conviction that they were a better side than most people suspected.

Harry Fearnley, their large and dependable goalkeeper, was a straight, blunt Yorkshireman who had joined Oxford that season after eleven years with Huddersfield. Cyril Beavon, at right-back, had been Turner's first signing, another free transfer, from Wolves, and was an indestructible defender who enjoyed an occasional gallop into the opposition half. Pat Quartermain, his full-back partner, was the only local boy in the side and a player who had first made his mark as a centre-half.

Maurice Kyle was considered one of the best centre-halves outside the First Division, a cool and efficient rock of a man who had also joined Oxford from Wolves and later attracted the attention of many other clubs. John Shuker was a Mancunian who had been recommended to the club as an outside-left and then played in various other positions for the Reserve and 'A' teams before settling down at left-half.

Oxford's right-winger Peter Knight had joined the club from Nottingham Forest in 1960 and was the fastest man in the side, a man who could make ordinary full-backs look desperately bad and a man, too, who could score goals; he had found the net five times in five games at the start of the season. Arthur Longbottom, once of Queen's Park Rangers, Port Vale and Millwall, was a quick, busy inside-right who sometimes promised more than he achieved in the penalty box – and who also changed his name by deed poll to Langley. 'Longbottom is real Yorkshire', he told his colleagues, 'and I've settled in the south now.' He was Langley in private, Longbottom on the football field.

Bill Calder was always a nagging threat at centre-forward, a sturdy, forceful Scot who had played for Leicester and Bury and cost Oxford their biggest fee, £8,000. The inside-left spot belonged first to Alan Willey and then Tony Jones – Willey a tall westcountryman whose goal – scoring ability had impressed Oxford when he played against them in a Cup-tie, Jones a wing-half by inclination but who discovered that as an inside-forward he had a knack for doing the right things on the big occasion. Willey was sharp and erratic, Jones more deliberate but, given a little room, a strong finisher. The baby of the side, just twenty, was Colin Harrington on the left-wing, and what he lacked in experience he made up for with his aggressive, nicely controlled running.

The Cup run began gently and continued unpromisingly. Folkestone, who that season were to win promotion from the

First to the Premier Division of the Southern League, were beaten 2-0 in the first round, a comfortable and well-rounded victory which United expected to repeat when they were again drawn at home to non-League opposition, this time Kettering Town who were in the process of being relegated from the Southern League's Premier Division. It proved, however, to be a hard and close game, a ninety-minute scrabble, which left Oxford feeling distinctly uncertain about themselves and grateful to have won 2-1.

The third round brought a known quantity to the Manor, Chesterfield, who were fellow members of the Fourth Division but not a club in very robust health. They brought only two coachloads of supporters with them and even they did not seem to expect much. Their suspicions were well founded: it was another wild and uneven game which Oxford won with a goal by Willey after fourteen minutes. The city, though, was showing interest. Ten thousand people had watched the Kettering game and more than 9,000 saw the victory over Chesterfield.

The momentum was quickening and although Oxford did not draw a financial 'plum' in the fourth round, they did well enough: Brentford, who had won the Fourth Division championship the season before and were now in the middle of the Third, were to be the next visitors to the Manor. United's luck in being drawn at home again was almost taken for granted, and everybody stressed knowingly that they had not lost an FA Cup-tie at the Manor since Arthur Turner's arrival five years before.

This time the crowd was more than 15,000 and they saw a hard and wholly engaging Cup-tie which Oxford were unfortunate not to win at the first time of asking. Twice they were a goal down but twice they equalized – the second time through the eager Willey – and then came painfully near to scoring a winner on several occasions in the last half-hour. But a replay was necessary and so Oxford had to travel at last.

By now, however, the city of Oxford was almost convinced that its football club was a worthy cause. Five thousand supporters headed for West London three days later, swelling the crowd at Griffin Park to 26,000. They saw Brentford control the early stages of the game and take an early lead, but

United then settled down, contained Brentford for a while and finally mastered them, with Calder scoring twice. It was a splendid Cup-tie which the *Guardian* described as 'lusty and dashing' and the *Daily Sketch* as 'a rollicking, rumbustious and royal affair.'

Oxford United's supporters had seen enough: they were now convinced their team was unstoppable. John Parsons of the *Oxford Mail,* and later of the *Daily Mail* and *Daily Telegraph,* was a reporter closer than any to United at the time and he remembers that night vividly. 'Everything seemed to take off', he recalls. 'Before and after the match the A.40 and the Henley Road were full of cars with Oxford registration numbers, you could hardly move for them, and at the end of the game every pub in the Brentford area seemed to be taken over by Oxford supporters. It was instant party-time, songs, beer, laughter, boasts . . . it was astonishing what effect that win had.'

One reason, of course, was that Oxford's fans already knew who their team would be meeting in the fifth round. The draw had been made twenty-four hours earlier and the prize for victory at Griffin Park could hardly have been grander. Blackburn Rovers were a First Division club with an illustrious past and a highly promising present: they were one of the teams of the season and very big news. The city of Oxford, still dreaming, was immediately stricken with a savage attack of Cup fever.

Arthur Turner received two dozen personal requests for tickets within an hour of the end of the game at Brentford and, starting next morning, the Manor took its place alongside the Bodleian and the Cherwell, Balliol and Magdalen and the rest of the City's major institutions. The club's directors met within twenty-four hours and decided the match would be an all-ticket affair limited to 20,000. Extra standing room would be provided alongside the Beech Road stand and at the Cuckoo Lane end, and tickets would be on sale from the following weekend, one per person with special measures taken to prevent forgeries.

United's staff were overrun. There were only three months left to the end of the season but supporters clamoured to buy season tickets at the full price of £7 7s, to make sure they would be there on the day Blackburn came to town. The club's telephone became so busy it surrendered. Ken McCluskey, their tall, affable secretary at the time, remembers: 'There were moments when the 'phone actually seemed to become hot. I thought it was going to melt. When it broke down the peace was sensational. All I said to everyone in the office was 'If the players can keep going, so can we".'

Ten thousand tickets were sold in two hours the following Sunday morning. Some fans had taken their places the previous evening and, having got their precious ticket, they then dashed back to the end of the queue which at one point was a mile long. Tents were erected, candles flickered and cards were dealt endlessly. Impecunious students stood alongside well-heeled motor-workers. A canny hot-dog seller spent the night there and probably made his fortune. Two men waited in the queue at the children's turnstile. 'Our boys are in a church choir', they explained, 'and they said they wouldn't go this morning unless we queued up and got them a ticket.'

There was endless speculation about the team Arthur Turner would choose. Ron Atkinson had missed the Brentford games because of a fourteen-day suspension, the price he paid for a moment of folly during one of the Christmas matches, and when he returned to the side for a home League game against Workington a week before the visit of Blackburn he had one of his 24-carat 'stinkers'. Atkinson, though, was a certainty, and there was more pointed talk about 21-year-old John Shuker who had performed splendidly in the two games against Brentford, Tony Jones who could play at wing-half or inside-forward, and Alan Willey who had hit a lean patch after his vital goals in the earlier rounds.

Turner kept his thoughts to himself and went to watch Blackburn play Nottingham Forest at Ewood Park the week before the Cup-tie. Blackburn won by 2-0 but Turner returned to say: 'I think I saw enough to convince me how we must tackle our task on Saturday.' In fact, Turner had made up his mind about his team to face Blackburn while he was driving back from Lancashire, but he did not announce it until the day before the match. But there was one thing about which Turner did speak out. Rumours were growing that one or two big clubs were showing a strong interest in some of his players – and Turner, repeatedly and emphatically, insisted that not one of his regular team was for sale . . . 'unless someone comes along with an argument which we are unable to ignore'.

Oxford's players trained for the Blackburn tie as they did for any other game, every morning plus a couple of afternoons, but there was nothing ordinary about the week itself. It was not every Monday, for example, that the players were asked to help set out dozens of forms inside the boundary wall to provide extra seats. It was not often, either, that television, radio and the national Press lived at the ground. Reporters queued up to interview Turner. If a player raised an eyebrow it was filmed for posterity, if another blew his nose it was described in immortal prose. It was only at Cup-time, too, that an anonymous supporter sent the players a sprig of white heather: the one for the Blackburn game arrived in good time and Tony Padley, the steward of United's neat little Supporters' Club, pinned it up behind his bar.

There were one or two fitness problems – what would any Cup week be without them? Jones had a couple of stitches in a small forehead injury received the previous week, and Shuker's temperature rose and there was a passing worry about 'flu. Blackburn, for their part, knew already that they would have to get by without the injured Keith Newton, a full-back who it was rightly being said would one day play for England. His place was given to Walter Joyce, a 27-year-old utility defender, who had just been bought from Burnley for £12,000.

Then, at last, Turner named his side; and it would have been surprising had it not contained a surprise. Willey was dropped, Shuker moved from right-half to left to make way for Atkinson, and Jones pushed forward from his customary left-half spot to take Willey's place at inside-left. Jones had his stitches removed the day the team was named and it was only the second time that season he had played in attack. Willey had his champions but, all in all, it was granted that 'Arthur probably knows best.'

The first sounds in Oxford on the day of the match, February 15th, 1964, were made by Blackburn supporters. Their coaches began to arrive in the half-light of a grey dawn and their bells and rattles shattered the serenity of a deserted city. They invited local residents to share their pleasure in a new day by pushing letter-boxes open and bellowing 'Good morning.' Dozens more gathered outside Woolworths singing 'Why are we waiting?' . . . and then, as the doors opened at nine o'clock, they scrambled inside to the cafeteria.

Crowds began to gather outside the Manor Ground at ten o'clock and with them arrived touts offering 5s ground tickets at 45s each and 10s stand seats at £6. They looked and sounded like men who could not be offended – until, that is, an elderly gentleman turned up clutching at least fifty tickets in his hand which he proceeded to sell at face value.

The gates opened at 12.20 – twenty minutes later than promised – but inside the Esso Caledonian Pipe Band was waiting to do its stuff, cheer-leaders hung onto strings of balloons which floated above them like huge bunches of grapes and a man in a skirt, amply padded blouse and red wig carried a banner round the ground with mounting pace and fervour.

A big, good-natured crowd waited patiently outside for Blackburn; and when the great men of the First Division arrived they were applauded and cheered respectfully as royalty or the prime minister might have been. The waiting fans pointed and whispered as they picked out Ronnie Clayton, captain of Blackburn and once of England, thirty-five times an international, a neat, dark man and a polished and constructive wing-half. The murmur rose again as they spotted Bryan Douglas with his spikey quiff of hair, a man who had played for England on thirty-six occasions, once one of the cleverest and most entertaining right-wingers in the game but now a schemer of guile and variety.

They recognized the tall, dark figure of Fred Pickering, who was considered one of England's finest prospects at centre-forward; he had recently scored a hat-trick for England's Under-23 side against Scotland and, only a week or so before the Cup-tie, he had scored all four goals in a 4-2 win by England's 'shadow' players over the first-choice international team. Close to Pickering, as Blackburn filed through, was the even larger and more powerful figure of Mike England who was rated by many as the finest centre-half in Britain, a Welsh international who was later to play with huge success for Tottenham and later still to manage Wales with distinction.

Others they were not too sure about, men such as Fred Else, the former Preston goalkeeper, an England 'B' player and a safe, wonderfully consistent performer; Mick McGrath, their busy left-half, and inside-right Andy McEvoy, two Republic of Ireland internationals; and the England Under-23 winger Mike Harrison, who had joined Blackburn from Chelsea. John Bray was there, too, a right-back from a famous footballing family, and so was Mike Ferguson, a solid and often effective left-winger who had been signed from Accrington Stanley – the side Oxford had replaced in the League. Clayton, Douglas, McGrath and Bray were survivors from the Blackburn side which had reached Wembley in 1960.

They looked, to the supporters of Oxford, a team of superior mortals. What those supporters did not know was that Blackburn were a club that had become twitchily obsessive about winning something. They had been called 'unfashionable' too often, they had flattered to deceive too often, and now that they had such a good team, their best for years, they were worried in case they again failed to win a pot of some kind.

Blackburn had been impressive in the two previous rounds, beating Grimsby by 4-0 and Fulham by 2-0, but their manager, Jack Marshall, warned his players about taking their Fourth Division opponents lightly. 'They're a big, hard, long-kicking outfit', he told them. 'They've a lot of power and they'll go at you. You'll realize after five minutes that they won't be a push-over.'

Others were less cautious. William Westall, writing in the *Blackburn Times,* had no doubts: 'Barring what would be a football freak, the Rovers would seem to be as good as through to the last eight. Everything points to it: class, technique, a commanding defence which has not conceded a goal in the competition, an England-rated leadership of attack and the country's cleverest schemer . . . I cannot remember any Rovers' pairing with a team about whom so little is known. Only Oxford's manager Arthur Turner rings a bell.'

A crowd of 21,700, who had paid £5,600 for their tickets, watched as Ron Atkinson won the toss and chose to defend the London Road end. *Oxford United:* Fearnley; Beavon, Quartermain; Atkinson, Kyle, Shuker; Knight, Longbottom,

Calder, Jones, Harrington. *Blackburn Rovers:* Else; Bray, Joyce; Clayton, England, McGrath; Ferguson, McEvoy, Pickering, Douglas, Harrison.

Blackburn were expected to win, but they knew that the cameras of the BBC, ITN and Pathe News, twenty-four reporters (myself among them) and twenty photographers were not there because they believed the result to be a foregone conclusion. It was a feeling which contributed to their nervous start and anonymous performance. Eric Todd summed up their afternoon in the *Guardian:*

> Blackburn were never allowed to settle down, and if they thought the long pass down the centre and to the wings would embarrass Oxford, they were soon disillusioned. Pickering waited 15 mintues for his first opportunity to shoot, and if he had another after that I did not see it. Douglas was clever and selfish in turn, McEvoy roamed unhappily and aimlessly, and speed on the wings counted for nothing. Behind, England and McGrath worked hard, and Joyce justified his inclusion as Newton's deputy, but at no time did Blackburn present a picture of potential Cup finalists or League champions presumptive. Individually they had their moments, collectively they had none. Their initial surprise and final dejection were pathetic to behold.

It was, gloriously, Oxford's day. They showed utter contempt for Blackburn's record and glossy reputation, and their margin of victory, 3-1, faithfully reflected their hold on the game.

Oxford neutralized the threat of Douglas early on and that was one of the keys to it all. No matter which way he turned, ran or passed, there was always United gold and black. He would beat one, even two, men in the course of his darting little runs but always there was a long Oxford leg to stop him before he could turn threat into danger. Soon there was frustration on his face, then anger, and his team suffered as a unit. They were a ship without a rudder.

Arthur Turner's plan had been for Jones, the third wing-half in his side, to mark Douglas – but Oxford found themselves in such command that their tactics naturally reshaped themselves. The tall, square-shouldered Jones, far from denying freedom to someone else, found he had freedom himself. The marker now had to be marked and Jones, skilfully avoiding the challenges of Clayton, responded gratefully by scoring the first two of Oxford's goals.

The first came in the fourteenth minute after Shuker with a throw-in and Knight with an incisive pass had started a movement along the right. Longbottom centred, low and hard, England just failed to intercept, a shot by Calder was blocked but not cleared, and Jones – on his own – drove firmly into the net. Seven minutes into the second half Atkinson sent a long ball from the right towards the far post, Calder nodded it down and Jones – still on his own – used his right foot to score easily and emphatically. 'We want three', bellowed the Oxford fans, and after Ferguson had given Blackburn a fleeting glimpse of hope with a goal through a cluster of defenders in the 69th minute, the Manor got its wish. A telling pass from Quartermain found Calder in splendid isolation just a minute from the end and he took the chance with relish.

The triumph was a collective one, a product of enthusiasm, guts and honest-to-goodness skill, in which the half-back line above all excelled itself. Atkinson was a phenomenon, a captain who led with fire and by example, covering endlessly, tackling sharply, anticipating cleverly and distributing wisely. He did the work of about three men and was a force with which Blackburn never came to terms. Kyle got the better of Pickering, resolutely but stylishly, and long before the end the Blackburn centre-forward was showing his frustration by shouting uncharitable things at every colleague who came within ten yards of him. Shuker, too, was a major influence, making life thoroughly uncomfortable for McEvoy, contributing to Douglas's lean afternoon and giving Jones his match-winning freedom in front.

The Manor crowd cherished every second. Director Fred Jones munched his way furiously through a pound of toffees, a publican screaming 'Ox-ford, Ox-ford' lost his false teeth and couldn't find them, two women behind me cried on each other's shoulder and – every time a goal was scored or nearly scored – people stood on their seats waving mortar boards.

The noise in the closing minutes was so overwhelming that

only a handful of players could have heard the final whistle. It was the signal for most of the crowd to pour onto the pitch. The gold shirts of the Oxford players disappeared without trace until Atkinson was suddenly lifted up, a flash of colour above the bobbing heads, and chaired around in triumph. The fans even began to dance – led by a woman (I think it was a woman) with orange hair, orange blouse and socks, blue skirt and a wealth of gold and black ribbons. The police looked on like happy uncles.

Champagne was waiting for the players in their shanty dressing-room and soon they were joined by Arthur Turner who looked as if he had been embraced at least twice by every spectator in the ground. 'Can you tell me', he shouted, 'how in the most important game in our history you all hit your best form and produce the best game we've ever played. You matched quality with quality . . . I'll tell you, lads, I just sat there rubbing my eyes to make sure it was true.'

John Parsons, who is a qualified referee and not a writer given to overstatement, informed his *Oxford Mail* readers that the victory was 'magnificent, memorable and almost miraculous . . . this was no ordinary Cup shock with the underlings sneaking success from the masters, but an impressive, clear-cut and exhilarating triumph by a superior side.'

The *Oxford Mail* did the occasion proud and even sent their drama critic, Don Chapman, to the match. He reported: 'I would not dare to assess the technical merits of this famous victory, but certainly in the theatre I have never been seized by my neighbour and kissed on both cheeks as I was by an unknown young lady when Tony Jones sent the crowd into ecstasy . . . the game was just as intense and had a pattern of inevitability which many a playwright would give his ears to achieve on the stage . . . as drama it was in the classic mould.'

The *Blackburn Times,* understandably, was less enthusiastic. On its front page it announced simply: 'R.I.P. . . . in memory of the Rovers' Cup Dream.' Inside, it described the defeat as 'a national sensation and a Blackburn disgrace that is going to take years to live down.' An anonymous supporter sent every member of the Blackburn side an 'In Memoriam' card.

The draw for the quarter-finals gave new substance to Oxford's dreams. They were drawn at home for the sixth round in succession and again their opponents were a famous Lancashire club, Preston North End. Preston, though, belonged to the Second Division – they were in third place, maybe, but still only in Division Two, and hadn't United already beaten one of the best teams in the First?

Oxford's momentum built up again. The clamour for tickets was so intense that secretary Ken McCluskey even invited the noisiest critics to join him in his office. 'I am perfectly prepared to sit back and watch them have a go at their own peril', he said. Once again, too, there was a wealth of eccentric stories, the daftest of all a claim by one of United's directors, John Hamilton, that the club owed their success to a chubby little Chinese figure called Ho-Tei which he had bought in a junk shop. Pictures of Ho-Tei clearly showed him to be laughing his head off.

Ron Atkinson, for his part, thought that the Manor Ground supporters would have rather more influence on the result than an Oriental idol. 'When Preston hear our crowd', he said, 'they'll think it's the Spion Kop at Liverpool.' Ray King, United's trainer, had been Port Vale's goalkeeper in 1954 when as a Third Division club they reached the semi-finals – and King said Oxford's forward line was a better one than Port Vale had. The club's gold-fronted programme for the match offered some relevant facts of its own: 'North End have long been notorious for their tendency to be knocked out of the Cup by opponents in a lower grade than themselves, and they have suffered such defeat six times since the war, their conquerors in every case being Southern League sides. They were also knocked out of the Cup in the SIXTH ROUND twice in the last four seasons, and seven times in the last thirty years. That sixth round is a regular bugbear to them. Could it be the same today?'

Preston's manager Jimmy Milne, meanwhile, was saying quietly that they had 'learned lessons' from Blackburn's defeat by Oxford. They had sent Tom Finney, one of the great men of Preston and football, to watch Oxford lose a League game at Halifax the week before – and they arrived at the Manor well informed, well prepared, confident but not over-confident and with their captain Nobby Lawton, the former Manchester

United wing-half, declaring 'What we get we shall have to earn, every man of us.'

Oxford again had a full house and an international audience. A Russian radio commentator joined the ranks of the media claiming he had ten million listeners and, less glamorously, dozens of fans without tickets stood precariously on lofty scaffolding erected just for the game outside the ground. Preston brought their own prancing cheer-leaders and Oxford paraded a four-foot-high silver cut-out of the Cup.

It proved, however, to be the day Oxford's luck ran out. Preston won the toss and chose to kick up the slope – which was United's preference – and fortune did not improve for the Fourth Division side. Alex Dawson, Preston's centre-forward, a dark, forbidding man of enormous power, put his side into the lead after only eight minutes with a goal that the City of Oxford still insists was offside – and rightly so. The Press box was a wretched temporary affair next to the dressing-rooms, close enough to smell the embrocation and a bad position from which to watch the game as a whole, but perfectly placed to see that Dawson was a yard offside as Alan Spavin, Preston's inside-left, pushed the ball through. Dawson scrambled the ball into the net, the linesman's flag stayed down and Oxford had their first intimation that Preston were going to be a problem.

Those suspicions were confirmed as Preston, looking unforgivably cool in their white shirts, played with relaxed confidence, using the ball as if they respected it and emphasizing that Cup football doesn't always have to be a form of warfare. Their belief in themselves was rewarded again just before half-time when Doug Holden, their England left-winger, angled the ball towards the edge of the Oxford penalty area and Brian Godfrey, their young Welsh inside-right, timed his move intelligently. He darted between Kyle, Beavon and Quartermain, and hit the ball on the run past the desperately advancing Fearnley. Preston were two up and the slope was going to be in their favour in the second half.

Football, however, is not an exact science. Its chemistry can change for all manner of reasons, and ten minutes or so after half-time the balance of power in the game began to change. Perhaps Preston began to fret a little under pressure, perhaps it was because Kyle was getting the hang of the marauding Dawson, perhaps Oxford stopped trying to match Preston at their own more articulate game. Whatever the reason, Oxford lost their hesitancy, their pace and thoughts quickened and the crowd, sensing that all might not be lost after all, got squarely behind them.

Oxford now threatened to devour Preston. There was nothing very subtle about the way in which they whacked the ball towards the Preston penalty area from every angle and at every height, but it soon produced a dividend. A long ball from Kyle was followed by a shorter lob by Atkinson and Jones, the hero of the Blackburn game, used his right foot to hook the ball in on the half-volley.

There was rather less than half an hour left and it belonged almost exclusively to Oxford. A venomous shot by Shuker was stopped on the line, Jones was fractionally wide, a header by Knight passed just over the bar, Longbottom touched another chance past a post and, the most palpable miss of all, Calder failed to make contact altogether after a perceptive pass from Shuker had found him only five yards from the Preston net.

The game moved into extra time with Preston in total panic. They were kicking the ball anywhere, their early assurance just a distant memory, and in the third and final minute of added time Oxford won three corners. Fans were screaming themselves purple and even policemen were shouting. Two supporters fainted and others turned their back on the mad scramble. The final whistle was needed to restore sanity and when it came it was almost a relief.

Oxford were out of the Cup and Preston instead were on their way to a Wembley final which they were to lose to West Ham. But Oxford had made their exit with robust dignity, and even before the players were out of the bath, Arthur Turner was realistically turning his thoughts to the future.

'We've started to move forward', said Turner. 'We've got a good side and I'm going to make it better. Now we want promotion.' The following season, 1964-5, they did go up; and three seasons after that, in 1967-8, they won the Third Division championship. United had moved from the Southern League to the Second Division of the Football League in little more than six years. That remarkable rise, and their famous victory over Blackburn, proved once again that in football all things are possible.

9 Colchester...1971

Dick Graham, the manager of Colchester United, a warm, honest and complex man, took a stroll down to the waterfront at Holland-on-Sea on the morning of Saturday, February 13th, 1971. That afternoon his Fourth Division team, 75th in the Football League and known affectionately as the Grandads' Army, were at home to Leeds United, clear leaders of the First Division, well-backed favourites to win the FA Cup and the UEFA Cup, and one of the meanest sides in Europe, in the fifth round of the Cup.

'I sat down on a bench and had a few moments to myself', recalls Graham. 'It was beautiful, just like a summer day, with blue sky and a calm sea. And as I looked out I knew, beyond all shadow of doubt, that we were going to beat Leeds. I can't tell you why – I just did. It wasn't wishful thinking. It was total conviction. I knew we were going to win.'

And Colchester did; by three goals to two. It was a defeat which defied logic, confounded the game's luminaries and earned the Grandads an indelible place in the story of the tournament. They even made front-page news on the day the nation went decimal and the bob, florin and noble half-crown passed into history.

William Jones, philosopher and non-footballer, once observed there was little difference between one man and another 'but what little there is, is very important.' The little differences between Leeds and Colchester were also plentiful.

Leeds' players were insured for £1,400,000; Colchester's whole team had cost £15,000. Leeds had nine internationals in their side: Colchester had one, Ray Crawford, who had played twice for England nine years previously. Leeds were at their peak: Colchester had seven players over thirty. Leeds were used to playing in the finest stadiums in Europe: Colchester shared with Cambridge the distinction of having the smallest crowd capacity, 16,000, in the League. In the previous two seasons

Leeds had attracted gate receipts of half a million pounds: four days before the Cup-tie Colchester announced a loss over the year of £17,400. Leeds' players, with handsome basic pay, numerous bonuses and innumerable extras, were among the best paid in the land: Colchester's top wage was £35 a week. Leeds were being quoted at 18-1 to complete a unique treble: Colchester were 100-1 and more just for the Cup.

These 'little differences' were emphasized again by a less than innocent question from Billy Bremner, Leeds' captain and Scottish international wing-half, when he heard the draw. 'Where', he asked, 'is Colchester?' Terry Cooper, their England full-back, then knelt down and put his head on the block. 'If we lose we should all be instantly sacked,' he said.

Bremner's uncertain grasp of geography was a mite less pardonable than Cooper's over-confidence. Colchester, after all, had been around for some time. It is England's oldest recorded town, an hour by rail to the east of London and, according to a soufflé-light English Tourist Board brochure, its early importance 'goes back to Shakespeare's Cymbeline – properly Cunobelin – who ruled over the kingdom of the south-east from a capital on the river Colne . . . here the Romans established their first colonia in Britain, as their new capital in A.D.50, to be burnt down by the patriot Queen Boudicca ten years later.' Colchester, in fact, is a garrison town which carries its age lightly, a place of good inns and curious names, timber-framed buildings and busy activities – though in its lengthy list of places to see and things to do the wretched brochure made no mention of Colchester's football club.

There was no reason why Bremner should have been versed in Romano-British history but he ought, perhaps, to have heard a whisper that back in 1948 – two years before they moved out of the Southern League and into the Football League – Colchester United had shown their teeth in another remarkable Cup-run. They beat Huddersfield of the First Division, whose side included the great Peter Doherty, and then Bradford Park Avenue, who were talented members of the Second. Colchester's success was happily attributed to secret plans and the magical properties of local oysters. Someone should also have mentioned to Bremner that no First Division club had ever beaten Colchester in a Cup-tie in the pinched confines of their ground at Layer Road.

Colchester, in their 21st year as a League club, were ready again for something special. Their manager, Dick Graham, a vital and intelligent sergeant-major of a man, had the club in perfect battle order. It was a small club, maybe, but it was a straight-backed, well groomed, fit, confident and campaign-hardened. Graham had poured his energies into the club, and his qualities were sharply and faithfully reflected by his team.

Graham, his military-short hair beginning to grey at the temples, was a Northamptonshire man who had been a goal-keeper with Northampton, Leicester and Crystal Palace, trainer-coach under Vic Buckingham at West Bromwich Albion and then managed Crystal Palace to promotion to Division Two. His style was highly individual: he trained his men like commandoes, sometimes until they dropped, he used every artifice imaginable to stimulate them and he was one of the first managers, perhaps *the* first, to get away from the old idea that the number on a player's back should tell you where he plays and what he does as well as identify him – 'my numbers game', he called it. He considered things like using a computer to build up a bank of information on every player in the League, he was an expert in the transfer market, a shrewd psychologist, a knowing publicist and a clever, unpredictable tactician. Not everything he tried succeeded, but he never followed in another man's steps. He was his own man; he made his own mistakes.

Graham's experience of Cup football was rich and varied. He had helped take West Bromwich to a semi-final replay and two quarter-finals, and then steered Crystal Palace to the quarter-finals in 1965 – at which point, oddly, they were beaten 3-0 by Leeds. Don Revie and his Leeds team were just emerging as a major power, and Revie and Graham met again as old team mates. They had played together for Leicester. It was a meeting – and a defeat – which Graham did not forget.

Grandads' Army was an elderly side of mixed pedigree. 'I did well out of a common managerial mistake, writing players off too early', recalls Graham.

When many players approach 30 they go through a natural stage when their game goes off a little, and this is when they need their manager's support to help them through. Too often they don't get it and they are passed on, yet the truth is they still have a lot to offer.

It meant I was able to get together a team full of players with wonderful experience with all kinds of clubs at all kinds of levels. Some had known the big-time, others only the Third and Fourth Divisions. It didn't matter because often there's not much difference between players at the top and bottom. Sometimes it's only circumstances or a bit of luck which decides where they land up. A good player can turn it on wherever he finds himself, and I knew that in my side I had players who on any one day, provided they played their own game and used the ability they'd been blessed with, could match the best.

Graham Smith, Colchester's goalkeeper, was a good example. He impressed Dick Graham when playing against Colchester in one of his ten games for Notts County and moved to Layer Road on a free transfer. A Liverpudlian and a physical-education teacher, Smith then developed during the next two seasons into one of the best 'keepers in the Fourth Division.

Bobby Cram, their captain and right-back, was another good, but different kind of example. He had been in the game sixteen years, twelve of them with West Bromwich Albion with whom he had twice appeared in a League Cup Final – in 1966 when they beat West Ham and twelve months later, the first League Cup Final to be played at Wembley, when they were beaten by Queen's Park Rangers. Cram later played for Vancouver Royals, a North American League side managed by the legendary Ferenc Puskas, but they folded and he became an insurance agent. Dick Graham remembered Cram from his own days at the Hawthorns and for the price of a telegram to Albion he acquired a ready-made leader and defender on a free transfer.

Brian Hall was Colchester's left-back and longest-serving player. He had been signed from Mansfield for £1,000 in 1964 as a left-winger; and even as a defender he still moved forward with pace and skill. John Gilchrist was a Scot who gave body and experience to Colchester's defence and had come from Fulham on a free transfer after a dozen years with Millwall.

John Kurila, a gentle soul off the field but a warrior of a centre-back on it, found his way to Layer Road via Celtic, Northampton, Bristol City, Northampton again and Southend. He played an important role in Northampton's dramatic rise from Fourth Division to First – but he was one more player for whom Dick Graham paid nothing. Brian Garvey, Kurila's partner at the heart of Colchester's defence, played more than 400 games for Hull and Watford, and was yet another free transfer.

Brian Gibbs, a versatile chap in midfield or attack, was a leading goal-scorer with Bournemouth and Gillingham before joining Colchester for £5,000. Another fee, £2,500, was paid for Brian Lewis, a busy, attacking player who had been with Crystal Palace (under Dick Graham), Portsmouth, Coventry, Luton and Oxford. Dave Simmons, once of Arsenal, Aston Villa and Bournemouth, also cost a fee, £5,000, and he provided height and muscular finishing power in front. He was to get an excellent service from Mick Mahon on the left-wing, another physical-education instructor who learnt the game with Port Vale and York before joining Colchester on a free transfer.

Then, of course, there was Ray Crawford himself. Crawford, tall, rangy, highly mobile and a lethal finisher, was one of the heroes of the Ipswich side which Alf Ramsey led to the championships of the Second and First Divisions in successive seasons in the early 1960s. He scored 203 goals for Ipswich, still a club record, but – a little unluckily – only played twice for England, against Northern Ireland and Austria in 1961-2, despite not being on a losing side and scoring in the second. Crawford led a busy life after those great years at Portman Road: he moved to Wolves, then West Bromwich, returned to Ipswich and, slowly winding down it seemed, he later moved to Charlton before drifting out of the League and joining Kettering Town. But Dick Graham was watching him closely and in the summer of 1970 he offered £1,500 to Charlton for Crawford's registration and another £1,500 to Kettering. Both clubs agreed, Crawford joined Colchester for £3,000 and the following season at the age of thirty-four he scored thirty-two goals for them.

Dick Graham looks back at his team with warm affection:

Graham Smith would have graced the First Division at any time and I really believe that . . . the crowd at Layer Road always loved the sight of Brian Hall overlapping, and what a wonderful left foot he had . . . Bobby Cram, a player who knew what it was all about . . . John Gilchrist, good marker, good discipline . . . John Kurila and Brian Garvey, lots of experience, plenty of heart, consistent players.

Brian Gibbs was what I have always called a seasoned Third or Fourth Division player, loyal, enthusiastic, a player who gave the team something, you could depend on him every match, home or away, to do his best . . . Brian Lewis, a player of tremendous ability, two-footed, a pin-point passer, very much like Ronnie Allen used to be; I bought him mainly to provide a service for Ray Crawford and Dave Simmons . . . Mick Mahon, another great left foot, a man who knew how to take corner kicks – we got so many goals from them that season – but he could also score himself. Mick and Brian Hall, our left-back, worked well together. Sometimes they'd run into each other and we'd all have a good laugh but we got so many telling things from them when they were working together.

Dave Simmons was a player I'd watched right from his days as a youngster with Arsenal, a big strapping lad with power in the air and a good shot . . . and what can I say about Ray Crawford. A wonderful bloke. I just admire people who can score goals.

Six of the team joined Colchester on a free transfer, five cost fees totalling £15,000 and together they added up to a force which, by the time they met Leeds, had lost only three of their previous twenty-four games and beaten Ringmer, a Sussex amateur club, Cambridge United, Barnet of the Southern Leage and Rochdale on their way to the fifth round of the Cup.

Rochdale alone provided stiff opposition. They met in the fourth round in front of a 12,000 crowd at Spotland; and although Crawford gave Colchester an early lead it was their Third Division rivals who then dominated the game. Inspired by Norman Whitehead, Rochdale moved firmly and intelligently into a 3-1 lead and the issue seemed settled. But Colchester fought back doggedly, made gainful use of a bit of

Leeds had already stepped beyond the wildest dreams of most clubs as they prepared to meet Colchester. They had won the League championship in 1969 and been runners-up in 1965, 1966 and 1970. They won both the League Cup and European Fairs Cup in 1968 and been beaten in ths FA Cup Finals of 1965 and 1970. The previous year, with only a few weeks of the season left, they had been chasing a tremendous treble, League championship, European Cup and FA Cup, but fell at one of the last hurdles in all three competitions. Here were the bones of Revie's success and failure. He had a team of winners who often finished second. Was the fault in the team? Or in Revie the manager? Or in Revie the man?

We can only guess at the answer but, in any case, Leeds were only failures by their own remarkable standards. As Dick Graham and his trainer, Denis Mochan, travelled to watch Leeds play Liverpool at Anfield on the Saturday before the Cup-tie, there was no doubt in their minds that they were going to run the rule over a side of singular excellence. Leeds had lost only one of their previous nineteen games in the League and were sitting comfortably on top of the First Division, three points clear of Arsenal and nine ahead of third-placed Chelsea. Colchester, for their part, were seventh in Division Four, thirteen points behind Notts County at the top.

Leeds, as it happened, lost at Anfield to a goal by John Toshack but that in itself was unremarkable: Liverpool did not lose a home game all season long. Graham, as he remembers, was looking past the result and into the heart of Revie's side:

> All teams, even the greatest, have a weakness somewhere. I knew all about Leeds and their qualities and I knew it was going to be hard to find a weakness – but I knew one had to be there. The trouble is that even if you spot a weakness you have still got to exploit it. You wonder if your own players can take advantage of it, or if the opposition are aware of it and are capable of covering it up. I was a great believer in playing the averages, though, and if I spotted a weakness, no matter how small, then I believed in playing on it over and over again in the hope of something giving way. Anyway, I did spot a weakness or two in their defence and I came away convinced that the blend of my team was just right to exploit them.

The names of the Leeds team ran off most tongues as easily as a popular nursery rhyme, though in the week before the Cup-tie it became increasingly apparent that Billy Bremner was losing his fight to recover from an injured ankle. His place in midfield was taken by Mike Bates, small, bravely committed, experienced and a wholly reliable stand-in.

Gary Sprake of Wales was in goal, a man whose rich talent was sometimes undermined by a curious twitchiness under pressure. He could make stunning saves and astonishing mistakes with equal facility. The defenders in front of him were England internationals to a man: Paul Reaney, a quick, positive right-back and an enterprising overlapper; Jack Charlton, one of Alf Ramsey's world-beaters in 1966, tall, angular, hugely experienced, a formidable opponent and a menace in the air when pushing forward for corners and free-kicks; Norman Hunter, the hardest man of a hard side, his tackle enough to demolish a brick wall; and Terry Cooper, a left-back of such skill and adventure that he looked exactly what he was, a former left-winger.

Leeds' key man in midfield, particularly in Bremner's absence, was Johnny Giles of the Republic of Ireland, strong, undentable and just 5ft 5ins tall, a craftsman of subtlety and infinite variety and a man who shaped every game in which he played. Alongside him there was Bates, who was well versed in the Leeds style, and Paul Madeley, a tall, powerful athlete and an astonishingly accomplished all-rounder who was to win his first England cap at the end of the season.

Peter Lorimer of Scotland on the right-wing was a forthright attacker with one of the hardest shots in football and alongside him were two more England internationals, Allan Clarke and Mick Jones. Clarke was lean and straight, a man with a nose for space and opportunity and the ability to finish with stealthy accuracy, while the basis of Jones's game was courage, nicely harnessed power and selfless running. It was by any count a formidably equipped side, gifted, subtle, well-integrated, hard and not blessed by an outsize conscience.

They were always thoroughly prepared, moreover, and forty-eight hours before the Cup-tie they took part in an all-out practice game at Elland Road in which they simulated what they imagined would be 'Colchester conditions' – flying tackles, feverish running, long, high balls and bruising contact. As always, too, Don Revie ran through the Colchester team in detail, their strengths and weaknesses and everything in between.

Dick Graham respected Don Revie's professional relish for detail but, looking back, he still believes that knowledge is sometimes a factor which gives a small club an advantage over a major rival:

> The big club may not know as much about you as you know about them. You see them regularly on television, hear about them and read about them. They probably have to check up on the names of the players in your side, names they might never have heard before, and although they send someone to watch you once or twice they can't be sure what they're looking at. Teams can change from match to match, individuals or even whole sides can play above or below themselves, tactics can change, opponents change, conditions change. It was easy for me to come to conclusions about Johnny Giles and Allan Clarke, say, but with respect to my players what did Don Revie really know about Mick Mahon or Brian Hall? It might have made a small but important difference.

Leeds emphasized their thoroughness by flying down for the game, a 55-minute flight from Leeds to Woodbridge instead of a five-hour train journey, and then travelled by coach to Clacton where they stayed at the Royal Hotel. Colchester, for their part, stayed at Holland-on-Sea, a couple of miles up the road, at what they considered their lucky hotel, the eighteen-room Kingscliffe, where they had prepared for all the previous rounds.

On the morning of the match some of the Colchester players put on their tracksuits and loosened up on the beach, others went for a quiet walk and Graham himself sat on a bench and became convinced – 'beyond all shadow of doubt' – that his team were going to win. He was, though, still to have an attack of nerves. He followed the team coach to Layer Road in his car and as the ground came into sight he admits he had 'a sudden attack of butterflies'. Would his team play as he knew they could? Would they get stage fright in front of a packed house? His nerves were quietened the moment he entered the home dressing-room. His players were calm and confident. They looked like men who knew what they had to do.

Graham had considered his tactics carefully:

> I gave two of our players a 'special' job but I insisted that the rest played their normal game when it came to covering space, responsibilities, switching, set-pieces and so on. I knew it would be wrong to change things for that one match – no matter how different or big the problems. I emphasized all the time that if they played their own way and did their talent justice they would be fine. The two 'special' jobs went to John Kurila and John Gilchrist. I asked Kurila to do a man-for-man marking job on Allan Clarke and Gilchrist to move into midfield and take on Johnny Giles in the same way. If Clarke and Giles went to the toilet I wanted my two men there as well.

Colchester United and Layer Road had never been better prepared for any match. The club printed 12,000 souvenir programmes with a simple but attractive cover of green and blue surrounding the Cup in silver and, inside, there were a dozen assurances that 'this is the day' – plus, prudently, nearly forty fund-raising advertisements. A hundred policemen were on duty, complete with mobile HQ and patrolling dogs, a detention centre was prepared behind the Layer Road stand, two ambulances stood by and thirty stewards were there to pack in a crowd of 16,000 which had paid a ground record of £9,500 for the privilege of being there.

The crowd itself was a bonus for the Colchester players. Their contracts entitled them to an extra £1 10s each for every thousand spectators in a Cup run. The Leeds players, as they took the field, saw a scene that looked somewhat less rewarding. Television cameras peered down from a huge platform opposite the main stand, leafless trees peeped at them from outside the ground and the mood of the place was raw and hostile. The pitch itself was obviously smaller than their own at Elland Road – six feet narrower and fifteen feet shorter in fact – but the proximity of the crowd made it seem the size of a tennis court.

Leeds were confident but wary, Colchester hopeful and determined, and the crowd noisy and just a little curious. No one knew quite what to expect. The teams lined up: *Colchester:*

Smith; Cram, Hall; Gilchrist, Garvey, Kurila; Lewis, Simmons, Crawford, Gibbs, Mahon. *Leeds:* – Sprake; Reaney, Cooper; Bates, Charlton, Hunter; Lorimer, Clarke, Jones, Giles, Madeley. Referee: Danny Lyden of Birmingham.

What happened then, simply, is that Grandads' Army fixed their bayonets and charged into a three-goal lead, through Crawford in the 18th and 24th minutes and then Simmons in the 55th, and although Leeds came back with steely professionalism to score through Hunter and Giles, the Fourth Division mix of rejects, hand-me-downs and OAPs hung on heroically to win 3-2.

Had Leeds started as they finished the outcome might never have been in doubt; but it was Colchester who got it right at the start and for most of the first hour, and the game was won and lost before Leeds remembered who they were and where they were. The First Division club's confidence was jarred and their rhythm disrupted. It was a situation outside even their experience and they responded with anxious muscularity rather than skill and familiar disciplines; and it cost them the game because Colchester had forwards in Crawford and Simmons who were good enough to punish the worst of their errors.

The *Colchester Evening Gazette* produced a special souvenir edition to mark the victory and it described the goals succinctly. The first from Crawford: 'Charlton was guilty of a clumsy tackle on Simmons right on the touchline and a rehearsed free-kick move brought that vital first blow. Lewis swung in the kick, Sprake, whose goalkeeping problems seem to increase with every match, came out and missed and Crawford ended with a superb header into the net.' And Crawford's second: 'Brian Gibbs, profiting from freedom on the right, swung in another high, tormenting cross, Crawford dived to head against Reaney's back and, while lying on the ground, collected the rebound to hook the ball as Sprake, too late, cottoned on to the danger.'

'Oddly enough,' recalls Graham, 'we didn't feel it was at all unbelievable. We went into our dressing room at half-time and it wasn't a case of everybody saying "Hey, we're two up against Leeds – how about that?" It wasn't like that at all. It was just like an ordinary League match. We'd done a good professional job – so far – but the game wasn't over. We knew we deserved to be two up but that was all there was to it. The game still had to be won.'

Ten minutes after half-time Colchester tightened their grip on Leeds' throat as, again in the words of the *Colchester Evening Gazette,* 'Crawford, still enjoying loads of freedom, started the move with a pass to Lewis who tossed up a high cross from the right. Sprake dithered and finally came but it was Simmons who was first there for another splendid header. Now the fantasy was true. . . '

The terraces were full of laughter, buzzing conversation and back-slapping. Many supporters in the stand were on their feet obliging the people behind them to climb onto their seats. No one now seemed in any doubt that Leeds were out of the Cup – except, that is, Leeds themselves. It was at this point, with disaster staring squarely into their faces, that they showed their real quality. Leeds were three goals down but, suddenly, dramatically, they took control of the game.

Dick Graham knew exactly when and why the balance of power changed:

> What changed everything was a change in tactics by Don Revie. Don switched Giles and Clarke. He pushed Giles forward and dropped Clarke back into midfield because he realized what I was doing. He was trying to break our man-for-man marking. I knew what our answer had to be. We had to get Kurila to go into midfield and stay with Clarke and Gilchrist to drop back and stick with Giles. They could have done it quite easily because Kurila was originally a wing-half and Gilchrist had been a defender. It was the simple, natural thing to do. So there I was, sitting on the touch-line, trying to attract their attention. But by now the crowd was going potty, absolutely mad. Anyone not there couldn't possibly imagine the noise. I tried everything to attract their attention, in fact anyone would have done, but no one could hear me, no one looked in my direction, no one came near us, and there was Kurila staying back and picking up Giles instead of Clarke and there was Gilchrist still in midfield and marking Clarke instead of Giles.

This was a different proposition altogether, of course.

Giles was different, smaller, a bit sharper. He drifted away and around the penalty area and Kurila started to lose him. The next thing we knew was that Giles and Lorimer were giving Norman Hunter the chance to pop one into the net with his head. 3-1. Then Leeds started coming from everywhere – Charlton, Reaney, they were all coming up – and, next moment, Giles himself was putting one in. And at that moment I could see it all sliding away. The last 15 minutes were the longest in my life. Leeds played some magnificent football, wonderfully controlled, some of the best I've ever seen.

Graham got his team to settle down at last, however, and they might even have scored again from two breakaways, one of which gave Crawford a chance to complete his hat-trick. He swung at the ball with only Sprake to beat – and miskicked hopelessly. 'I was simply too whacked!' he explained later. But if Crawford was the day's natural hero, the last act of heroism was left to Colchester's goalkeeper, Graham Smith. He saved superbly in the last minute from a header by Mick Jones, and admitted afterwards: 'It was pure instinct. It was too close to think. I just grabbed the ball and hung on.'

Referee Lyden blew the final whistle and the Layer Road crowd looked and sounded if they had all been welcomed through the Gates of Heaven. The Colchester players, too, acted with one mind. They ran straight for Dick Graham, an open gesture of admiration and respect, which the Colchester manager confessed later 'had touched him ridiculously'. Gilchrist spoke for all the Fourth Division club's players when he said: 'We made for Dick because of what he had done for us. He is the best any of us have ever worked for. He wanted us to win for our sake, not his. He can be brutal in training but it works.'

The crowd dissolved slowly and reluctantly, talking again about Crawford's goals, his predatory single-mindedness and strength in front of goal, the support he received from Dave Simmons, the probing crosses of Brian Lewis, which rained down on Gary Sprake and the heart of the Leeds defence like artillery fire, the nagging back-up work of Brian Gibbs and Mick Mahon, the last ditch save by Graham Smith and, too, of the fiercely controlled fight back by Leeds with Norman Hunter, above all, their inspiration.

Colchester's players sang 'Grandad . . . Grandad' in the bath. The door of the Leeds' dressing-room remained shut for a long time. At the BBC Radio commentary point, Dick Graham was telling me: 'I said I'd climb the Castle wall if we won – and I think I will. It is the greatest day of my life.' Crawford, followed to the microphone by every small boy in the crowd, came up to add: 'People said I was being cocky when I'd promised I'd score, but I've always done well against Leeds and I had one of those funny feelings that players get when the Cup comes along.'

The Leeds team eventually appeared, led by Jack Charlton who patted a reporter on the cheek and joked: 'Well, you've got something to write about now, haven't you?' A few paces further along the corridor the tall England defender was saying: 'Nobody will ever let us forget this defeat. It will come up year after year when the Cup comes around.' Norman Hunter emerged to add his thoughts: 'If this lot get a home draw on Monday, they're there, in the semi-finals. A Fourth Division side! After what they've done to us no one will fancy coming here.'

The newspapers, large and not so large, handled the story of Colchester's triumph with huge and happy relish. Bernard Webber in the *Colchester Express* held nothing back: 'This conclusively, exclusively, was the most incredible result in Soccer history.' Frank McGhee of the *Sunday Mirror* saw it as 'probably the greatest FA Cup upset of all time'. Brian James, reminding everyone that some grandads are livelier than others, told *Daily Mail* readers: 'Not since the 7th Armoured Division took a German sneer and proudly incorporated it into their badge – the Desert Rats – has an insult become so effective an inspiration.' Phil Brown of the *Yorkshire Evening Post* was still perplexed on the following Monday afternoon: 'What on earth went wrong? I put the question to the skipper, Johnny Giles. "I just don't know", he said. "I only wish I did. Every single thing we tried went wrong. We were nearly all off, and I don't know why." Altogether if you came from Leeds you just could not believe your eyes at Colchester.'

The following Monday there was a discernible murmur of disappointment at Lancaster Gate when Colchester were drawn away to Everton who had won the League championship for a seventh time the previous season by a remarkable nine points – with Leeds the runners-up. Everton at Layer Road would have been another tie conceived in Paradise. Colchester at Goodison Park was more than just a bit unfriendly; it was the Cup being downright hostile.

Colchester, nonetheless, had reached the quarter-finals on merit. Strange things happen in the Cup and 5,000 supporters, in special trains, coaches, cars and even chartered aircraft, followed Dick Graham's team excitedly up to Merseyside. The size of the Goodison crowd, 53,028, again reflected the irresistible appeal of the Cup and its giant killers. Colchester's faithful knew that Everton had players of the lofty calibre of Alan Ball, Howard Kendall, Colin Harvey, Joe Royle, Jimmy Husband, Roger Kenyon and John Hurst; but, then again, Leeds had not been a bad side either.

The Fourth Division club found Everton and Goodison Park a very different place from their own little world at Layer Road. It was much bigger and grander, of course, but they also felt it lacked some of the warmth that made their own club so happy. For one thing Colchester's young mascot, Michael Twiddle, was refused permission to the dressing-room area despite their wish that he should be. They also discovered that although there were six new-looking balls in the Everton dressing-room there were none in their own. They eventually found three old ones out on the pitch.

All this had nothing to do with the result of the game, however, and a very fine Everton side won the game with stylish ease by five goals to nil. Kendall with two, Royle, Husband and Ball scored their goals, four of them in a vital quarter-hour in the first half, and but for a splendid performance by Graham Smith in the Colchester goal there might have been one or two more. The Everton players applauded Colchester off the field; the crowd stood and Goodison Park rumbled its appreciation. It was a warm tribute and a dignified exit.

It was a season, in the end, which history remembers for two reasons above all. Colchester, yes, but it was also the season in which Arsenal completed the League and Cup double. They pipped Leeds for the title by just one point and beat Liverpool by 2-1 at Wembley. But it took Arsenal fifty-one matches to make their mark . . . Colchester needed only one.

10 Exeter... 1981

It took the Cup a long time to catch up with Exeter City but, when their moment came, it was worth the wait. City, just down the road from Exeter Cathedral, just up the road from the most roundly cursed bypass in Motordom and firmly based in the pastoral heart of the Third Division, were the last giant killers of the first hundred tournaments.

Exeter beat Leicester City of the First Division and then Newcastle, one of the most successful clubs in the multi-coloured story of the competition, to reach the quarter-finals for the first time in fifty years and only the second time in their history. They were stopped in the end by an international sweet-trolley of a team, Tottenham Hotspur, who went on to win the Cup.

It was a Cup run full of sweat and romance, engaging stories and stirring moments, rich humour and earthy reality, un-dentable committment and ever-flowering hope. The giant killers of the Cup could not have wished for a better postscript to their first hundred years of derring-do. A club from the small print of the game had again become the stuff of headlines. 'Wild West', bellowed one screamer in the size of type that usually terminates world wars. 'Apple-cider Heroes', offered another paper . . . 'Pride of the West' . . . 'Cream of Devon' . . . and, unbeatably, 'Exeter by-pass opens road to Wembley.'

Brian Godfrey, the sturdy and stable Welshman who managed Exeter through the four heady months of their Cup run, insists:

> It was headlines like that and all the other exposure we got, that will stick with us most of all. We got recognized and, never mind what others say, that is what the cup is all about. Instead of being just a club a long way from anywhere, just another possible draw on people's coupons, we were part of the national scene.
>
> Blokes in London were looking up Exeter in the timetables

> and coming to see us. We got big reports at the top instead of little paragraphs at the bottom. We were on television, 'Sportsnight', 'On the Ball' and all that. People knew what we looked and sounded like. We've all got pride, we wouldn't be in football if we hadn't, and the big treatment we got showed us the impact we were making on the country as a whole. We found we could take plenty of it.

It is all that Exeter and Devon stand for which made City's success so appealing. To the rest of this cluttered island the county is an attitude of mind, a shire that has more to do with a couple of week's hi-de-ho in the summer than professional sport in winter, a place of red soil and green hedgebanks, smock-and-straw accents and sheltered coombes. The people of Devon themselves see it through a slightly different window, but they are properly grateful that the Great Mapmaker used bolder strokes and brighter colours when he filled in their little corner of the world. Exeter City's success raised a smile on the face of the nation.

There was point and order to their Cup run. It jogged the memory and stirred the imagination. Leatherhead, Millwall and Maidstone, the clubs Exeter beat in the first three rounds, had all known the heady joy of giant killing themselves; and their opponents from that point on, Leicester, Newcastle and Tottenham, were all Wembley familiars. Exeter were drawn at home in the first round but then, their luck running out at Lancaster Gate, they were drawn away in the next five. But they still scored nineteen goals and conceded only seven in the eight matches that took them from first to sixth round. The two matches they drew, splendidly, were at Leicester and Newcastle. Only 4,600 people watched their first tie and even fewer, 3,400, their second . . . but 7,500 followed them across the broad base of England to White Hart Lane where an all-ticket crowd of nearly 41,000 saw them lose at last.

Few who warmed to Exeter's exploits in 1981 remembered the only other time the club had the audacity to force itself within two games of the Cup Final; but most City supporters were at least aware that in 1931 there had been an equally remarkable run. To a club which has spent its entire life in the League paddling away with spectacular lack of success in the

Third and Fourth Divisions, such moments are cherished above all. Their days in the League are as repetitive as a wallpaper pattern. It is the Cup which illuminates.

In Exeter's first charge towards Wembley, ten years after becoming one of the original members of the Third Division, they beat Northfleet, Coventry, Derby, Bury and Leeds, before drawing at Sunderland in the quarter-finals and then losing the replay on their own St James's Park by 4-2. It is part of the City's folklore, unchallengable gospel, that Sunderland should have been beaten. Percy Varco, their main goal-getter at the time, missed a gift of a chance at Roker Park and Arthur Davis, their goalkeeper, let in a sitter in the replay. Exeter have always known it was bad luck rather than bad play which stopped them then. They waited half a century for natural justice and 1981, it seemed, was to be the year.

Brian Godfrey's team may have been second out of the bag in five of the six draws in which they were involved, but on the field they made their own luck with methods as attractive and breezy as their own Devon coastline.

> We tried to attack, to push people forward, wherever we were (remembers Godfrey). Sometimes it was to the detriment of our defence but, really, we weren't equipped to get anywhere by laying back and waiting for something to happen. We were a very fair side: we had some good players who could have been doing well at a higher level, everybody worked and sweated and we had bags of pride and confidence. We knew we could do things and the longer the run went on the more we believed in ourselves. It was like a snowball.
>
> I know we are a remote club, a bit off the beaten track, but that worked for us in some ways. People in the game didn't see us at home. They didn't know what our ground and crowd were like – especially our crowd on big nights. When our place was full the noise and atmosphere was tremendous . . . fantastic. I couldn't see us losing. There was a wonderful togetherness. The team and the supporters were all part of the same thing.

Godfrey himself was only forty years old at the time of Exeter's Cup run, but his contribution was shrewd – level-headed judgement, driving ambition and a hefty volume of valuable experience. He had been an inside-forward or wing-half who played for Everton, Scunthorpe, Preston, Aston Villa, Bristol Rovers, Newport County, the American club Portland Timbers, and Bath City; a player, too, who was good enough to be capped by Wales on three occasions.

Godfrey's winding journey through football is reflected by his accent. Listen carefully and in addition to the lilt of his native North Wales, there is a dash of Brummie, a touch of Scouse, maybe a hint of the States and now, no question, a suspicion of the west country. 'A little bit of everything', he concedes. Managers, like everyone else, are the sum of their experience.

Cup football had certainly played its part in fashioning Godfrey. He has already played a part in our story, of course; he scored the goal for Preston which ended Oxford United's run in 1964. He was only Preston's twelfth man at Wembley that year, but seven seasons later he captained Aston Villa to the 1971 League Cup Final which Tottenham won with two fine, late goals by Martin Chivers.

Godfrey knew Cup football in all its moods, in moments of triumph and disappointment, on cramped provincial fields and grand stages, and he knew, too, that a Cup run did not begin and end with football. It filled every thought and hour and even pursued him to his home at Ottery St Mary, a dozen gentle miles to the east of Exeter. Once it even surprised him in the shower. The Lady Mayor of Exeter, Mrs Joan Richardson, called at the club's training headquarters at Woodbury to wish them well, arrived early and walked straight into Exeter's manager who was not even wearing aftershave. Godfrey, clutching an inadequate towel, moved faster than any of his players did all season long. 'The most interesting moment of my year of office', murmured Exeter's first citizen.

Exeter's team had been drawn from all corners and levels of the game for less than £200,000, its pieces fitting together uneasily to begin with, like an inexpensive jigsaw, but later bedding down with use and familiarity. Their backgrounds, talents and attitudes were oddly assorted but together they made good sense. Their characters developed like prints in a dark room as the Cup run picked up pace. Football followers talked knowingly of the Cornflake Kid, the Fastest Milkman in the West and the Rogers Cousins.

The Cornflake Kid was Peter Hatch, a tall, straight midfield player with a mop of curly hair who ate nothing but that particular breakfast food – maize, iron, added vitamins, sunshine, etc – before a match. Arthur Turner had signed him for Oxford as a sixteen-year-old but, after only nineteen games at the Manor Ground and already wondering if football held any future for him, he moved to Exeter in 1973. The job was steady, the money unremarkable but regular, the way of life pleasant and it was possible to stroll through Cathedral Yard or along Fore Street with his wife and young daughter without being mobbed by star-struck fans. Exeter City simply did not have stars . . . or at least they didn't until the Cup run. Then, at the age of thirty-one, Hatch found himself regarded as an authentic celebrity. His two good feet, unpredictability, occasional important goals and long throw were suddenly priceless commodities. It had taken him nearly sixteen years to become an overnight success. The Cup is capable of anything.

Ian Pearson, another member of Exeter's midfield, supplemented his football earnings by running his own milk-delivery service. He did not rattle his float into every dawn but on Sunday mornings – his regular start to the week – he found the Cup even softened the style of the notes left on some of his 300 doorsteps. 'Two pints', became 'Two pints and a goal please.' Pearson had reached the sixth round of the Cup once before, with Millwall in 1978, but he recalls that 'everything happened so quickly then . . . I enjoyed the Exeter run more because I was able to take it in my stride and enjoy it.'

The Rogers Cousins, full-back Martyn and forward Peter, usually found themselves interviewed together. Both were born in Bristol, both had played for Bath City; Martyn, the taller of the two, had once driven a lemonade lorry for a living, Peter had been a fitter with Rolls Royce. The Cup even let them share the biggest night of their workaday careers. They each scored a goal in the remarkable 4-0 victory over Newcastle . . . with the Cornflake Kid and the milkman scoring the other two.

The most celebrated member of the Exeter side, however,

was a Cornishman with thinning hair who less than five years before had been playing non-League football for Falmouth and working as a dockyard electrician. Tony Kellow was not only Exeter's leading scorer but for much of the season the most successful marksman in the League; a man, too, who in a roundabout way had helped put a smile on the face of Exeter's bank manager.

Kellow was spotted while playing for Falmouth against Exeter's reserves, enlisted at a modest cost of £1,500 and played his first League game for them at the age of twenty-four. Two successful years later Exeter sold him to Blackpool for £105,000 and sixteen months after that they bought him back for £65,000. It was a splendid piece of business.

Kellow began promisingly at Blackpool but when Alan Ball became manager there, after Stan Ternent and Bob Stokoe, there was a sudden reassessment of everything, a swishing of new brooms, and, according to Kellow, 'the atmosphere got very heavy, it weighed me down and I lost all my zest.' Godfrey and his righthand man, Malcolm Musgrove, the former West Ham winger, watched Kellow more than once and decided that although he looked only a shadow of the man who had left them they would take a gamble on the strength of what they knew. Kellow was ambitious, he still wanted First Division football, but he recognized the second chance Exeter were offering him.

The Exeter gamble paid off handsomely. 'We knew Blackpool hadn't seen him at his best and we knew that on first sight he didn't always look a thoroughbred', Godfrey explains. 'But we also knew this man would always score goals. He puts them away even when he's having a bad time. His record alone proves this. You can set your clock on him getting at least 20 a season.' Events were to prove just how well they knew their man.

Not even a Kellow can carry a team, however, and behind him he had substance and character. Len Bond, their elastic goalkeeper, was a westcountryman who had returned to his native acres after useful experience with Brentford. Two long-legged, durable men filled the heart of their defence: Phil Roberts was a Welsh international who had played for Bristol Rovers, Portsmouth and Hereford, and Lee Roberts (no relation) was a Wolverhampton man who had begun his career with Shrewsbury.

There was also a dash of old London Town in Exeter's make-up. John Delve, their resourceful captain, had been born in the west of the capital and started out with Queen's Park Rangers; and Dick Forbes, who completed Exeter's strongly manned midfield, David Pullar, who scored some vital goals when he played in the early rounds, and John Sparrow were also all Londoners. Sparrow, a £10,000 signing from Chelsea, arrived midway through the run and slotted in comfortably at left-back. Sparrow admitted he had thought Exeter was the end of the world – 'but they wanted me and that made all the difference.'

Godfrey often talked with pride about his 'team' but when he did he always meant more than just his players. He included Malcolm Musgrove, his other coach Alan Beer and, uniquely, two women physiotherapists. Polly Evennett and Anne Hansell, both in their early thirties, both pretty and both married, were in private practice in the town and got the job simply because they were good at it.

Dressing-rooms are not the coyest of places, but the players seemed embarrassed when they heard the news. 'You're pulling our legs, boss,' they said. 'No – but the girls will be', replied Godfrey. Polly and Anne pointed out immediately that they had seen men in every stage of undress and in every position possible, and soon they were accepted simply as two good physios. Godfrey remembers with a smile: 'To begin with I thought the players might start feigning injury just to get treatment, but once they'd seen how the girls could pound and pummel I got the impression some were backing off when they were genuinely hurt. The girls got players off the treatment table quicker than anyone I've ever known. They really knew their business.'

St James's Park, small and trim and surrounded maternally by narrow streets, did not get too excited about the first of Exeter's Cup opponents. Leatherhead of the Isthmian League had caused a stir themselves in 1975 by reaching the fourth round, but this time they were swallowed live by five goals to nil. Kellow scored twice and Pearson, Lee Roberts and an own goal by the Surrey club rounded things off for Exeter. Their reward was a second-round tie against Millwall, fellow but less successful members of the Third Division, at Cold Blow Lane in south-east London. The crowd was depressingly small, the game anonymous and a goal by Peter Rogers settled it. A good result away from home, nonetheless, and potentially a valuable one because it gave Exeter a place on the grid for the Third Round. They were lining up with the giants of the game. There was a chance of making a bob or two.

For half an hour or so Exeter fondly imagined themselves entertaining Liverpool or Arsenal or playing at Old Trafford or Villa Park; but in fact, when the draw was made that same Saturday evening to help the Pools companies with their pre-Christmas postal problems, they found themselves drawn away to Maidstone United or Gillingham. They then had to wait until the following Monday week, and a second replay, before knowing that Maidstone would be their next opponents. Exeter thus found themselves cast in the role of giants a long way from home and doughty Maidstone of the Alliance Premier League, having beaten one Third Division club, could see no earthly reason why they shouldn't beat another.

The afternoon, in all senses, proved splendid. The ground was clean and fresh, a crowd of more than 6,000 caring souls filled the stands and terraces, and the hamburgers on sale were delicious. Maidstone, a muscular side, even scored first, but Exeter kept pushing forward and their courage was handsomely rewarded. Goals by Pullar, who got two, Kellow and Peter Rogers saw them through by 4-2.

Exeter's luck in the fourth-round draw was mixed. They were drawn away again, which was unfortunate, but their opponents, Leicester City, were a First Division club which had reached the Cup Final four times in the post war years – and that was exciting. It was difficult, though, to assess Leicester properly.

They were managed, for example, by Jock Wallace, eight years the manager of Glasgow Rangers, a natural winner and a large, knowledgeable and demanding man, with a Scottish accent that made most of his countrymen sound like Laurence Olivier. Leicester were also a young side, average age twenty-one, and on their day, working hard and selflessly, well organized and full of running, they needed watching. They had already beaten Liverpool at Filbert Street. But it was still a fact of life that they were in desperate trouble at the bottom of the First Division, a side that found difficulty in scoring goals, in believing in itself and in maintaining any line of consistency. Their faults, perhaps, were the faults of youth. They were a side for the future – but not for the present.

On the day, as it happened, neither Leicester nor Exeter played well. Martin Henderson, tall and busy, a former Rangers player, gave Leicester an early lead, but Exeter, still pushing forward and making their luck, eventually earned a replay with a goal by Pullar. Godfrey talked afterwards about his side's mistakes, but sounded a happy man, while Wallace looked as if he wanted nothing more than a sharp claymore in his hand. 'He stormed into our dressing room afterwards and then had to walk out to avoid saying something he might regret', said a Leicester player.

It meant St James's Park could share in Exeter's Cup run once more, and on the night of the replay the old ground swelled with noise and pride. The crowd was just over 15,000 – twice their previous best of the season – and their faith was tangible, the atmosphere physical. The value of the prize helped, too. The draw for the fifth round had been made two days before and the winners would be away to Newcastle.

Exeter's players did not spoil things; there was never any doubt that it was their night. They played with zest and common-sense, cunning and unflagging committment, and Kellow, a hungry man, punished Leicester heavily for their defensive waywardness. A stranger dropping in would never have guessed which side carried the greater rank.

Kellow put Exeter in front after only ten minutes, moving smoothly onto a cross from Pullar, earning himself time and space and then shooting with studied care past Mark Wallington in the Leicester goal. Early in the second half, though it was more than they deserved, Leicester equalized, Jim Melrose making good use of one of the Exeter defence's rare mistakes and driving in a rebound. The Third Division club's reaction was immediate: they simply turned up the heat and Leicester, over-reacting, conceded a penalty . . . and Kellow, showing no sign of nerves, whipped the ball into the top left hand corner of the net. A few minutes later Kellow was again in the right place when he was needed. A corner from the left found its way through a filter of Leicester legs and Kellow gratefully completed his hat-trick. It was enough. Exeter had beaten a First Division club for the first time for fifty years and had reached the last sixteen for the first time since the Second World War.

Kellow moved like lightning as the final whistle went. He pounced on the ball, refused the referee's request to hand it over and announced for all to hear that 'this is one trophy I want to keep.' Jock Wallace, for his part, was manly in defeat: 'Once Exeter got back in front with the penalty the game was always going away from us. They deserved to win and I wish them good luck at Newcastle.'

The following week Leicester went to Anfield and beat Liverpool by 2-1 – the first time in eighty-five games over three years that the Merseyside club had lost at home. Leicester were also the first team to complete the League double over Liverpool for six years; and, in the month or so following their defeat by Exeter, Jock Wallace's team went on to beat Manchester United, Spurs and Arsenal and draw with Nottingham Forest. It did not save Leicester from relegation, but it stressed the essential worth of their young players and gave Exeter's achievement an extra coat of top-quality gloss.

The road was becoming steeper. Exeter now faced Newcastle and everything they stood for: the passion of the Geordies, Blaydon Races and their other sounds of war, the sustaining legends of men such as Hughie Gallacher and 'Wor Jackie' Milburn and, above all, their redoubtable record, six times winners of the Cup, eleven times finalists, four times League champions. Newcastle were taking part in the 100th Cup as a Second Division club but their past always lined up with the present. Kellow voiced Exeter's respect for the great Newcastle tradition when he said: 'The most important thing is that we play well enough to make sure the game doesn't pass us by. If we freeze we'll get slaughtered.'

Both clubs played on a ground called St James's Park – with St James's Street running alongside the Newcastle version and St James's Road flanking Exeter's home. They were separated, however, by much more than 350 miles of motorway. The real distance between them lay in their size, support, traditions and achievements. Newcastle mattered in the Cup: Exeter did not.

It was the first time, moreover, that the two clubs had met in a competitive match and nobody on Tyneside chose to remember that at the start of the previous season Newcastle had lost a friendly match at Exeter. St James's Park was full to its 38,000 capacity and on a still, almost peaceful day it could be sensed that the Geordies not only wanted victory – they needed it. Newcastle's manager Arthur Cox knew why. 'Times are hard up here,' he said, 'and football plays a major part in the way of life. Life on the dole is not much fun, which is why I hope we do well.' Exeter's following, a spirited 2,000, fought a losing battle as they tried to establish their identity.

The imbalance on the terraces was reflected on the field for much of a game that was ridden with anxiety and mistakes. Newcastle looked the better-equipped side, but their finishing was erratic and strain began to cut into the faces of some of their younger players. Stuart Boam, Newcastle's captain and burly centre-half, was already spitting out harsh words as his team returned to their dressing-room at half-time.

Twelve minutes into the second half, however, all was forgiven as the pint-sized Alan Shoulder, who had come on as a substitute in the first-half for the injured Bobby Shinton, gave them the lead. Alan Oliver, reporting in the *Newcastle Evening Chronicle's* Saturday 'Pink', described the goal like this: 'Shoulder himself had been fouled just outside the penalty area by Phil Roberts and the free-kick fell to Walker. The midfield man chipped a perfect ball into the middle where Shoulder got in a looping header from 12 yards which dropped over the top of Bond and into the net. It was only Shoulder's third goal of the season and his first since September.' Shoulder, a former pitman and the smallest player on the field, looked as if he was experiencing the single greatest moment of his life.

The Times picks up the story: 'Some of the mightiest sides in the land, having conceded a goal at Newcastle, have been known to fold their tents and quietly steal away, grateful that the injury suffered was not worse. The large crowd expected Exeter to do the decent thing and admit defeat. But instead of collapsing Exeter took the fight to their mighty opponents with admirable pluck and persistence and scored an unexpected but well-deserved equalizer four minutes from the end.' The scorer was Lee Roberts who put the ball into the net from close-in, following a long throw and a rare mistake by Newcastle's twenty-year-old defender Bruce Halliday. It was a goal that silenced Tyneside.

Arthur Cox insisted he was not 'too disappointed' and added, with curious timing, that his main job was to rebuild his team and create a better morale and happier atmosphere within the club. Then, more predictably, he added: 'The tie is still there for us to win. We had five good chances to Exeter's two and don't forget we had one disallowed, another kicked off the line and their 'keeper made some good saves.' Brian Godfrey, having watched his team hang on by their fingernails once again, added: 'I was a player under Arthur when he was a coach at Aston Villa and I know how well he will prepare his side for the replay.'

Tickets for the replay suddenly became more important than banknotes, marriage certificates and mortgage documents. The demand was going to be overwhelming, and the couple of thousand City fans who went to Newcastle knew this better than anybody. They arrived back home, bleary-eyed and travel-lagged, at two or three o'clock in the chill of the following Sunday morning and, instead of heading for bed and bath, many went straight to the ground where they queued until the club started selling tickets at ten.

Now it was Newcastle's turn to travel 350 miles, and the other St James's Park waited for them with a mixture of awe and excitement that turned into a hopeless case of Cup fever at its best and worst when the draw for the sixth round was made at lunch-time on the following Monday. Exeter and Newcastle – sharing the ball numbered eight – were the very last to be pulled out of the bag . . . and the prize was a game with Tottenham Hotspur at White Hart Lane!

Godfrey did his best to quieten things down – 'We are putting Spurs right out of our minds until after the replay', he said – and properly concerned himself with more immediate matters such as the fitness of one or two of his players, among them Kellow who was troubled by a hamstring injury. The Exeter players would have taken the field on crutches if necessary, however, and the side was at full strength when they lined up before an almost hysterical full house of 17,668. The teams: *Exeter* – Bond; M. Rogers, L. Roberts, P. Roberts, Sparrow; Forbes, Delve, Hatch, Pearson; P. Rogers, Kellow. *Newcastle* – Carr; Carney, Boam, Halliday, Johnson; Walker, Trewick, Wharton; Shoulder, Clarke, Waddle.

On the terraces the fans had been reading a programme note emphasizing Newcastle's previous embarrassments in the Cup. Hereford, Bedford, Peterborough, Hendon, Chester and Bury are among the names which haunt every redblooded Geordie; and it soon became horribly obvious to the 2,000 who had travelled in hope down to the west country that Exeter were about to join that list.

Exeter were inspired; their fans were thunderously behind them. The Third Division team attacked in heavy, rolling waves, battering at the Newcastle defence, forcing mistakes and then finishing with imagination and clinical accuracy. Donald Saunders of the *Daily Telegraph* saw it like this:

> Newcastle clearly were not prepared for the exhilarating football their opponents produced. Trewick, Wharton and Walker just could not cope in midfield with the busy Forbes and Delve. So Exeter were able to drive forward relentlessly, through the centre and along both flanks. Ultimately, even the experienced Boam could not hold his defence together . . . Exeter played with a skill, vigour and confidence one so rarely sees nowadays – even when giant killers are involved in Cup replays.

The goals came dramatically, the first direct from an inswinging corner by Peter Hatch after only fourteen minutes. Kevin Carr, the Newcastle goalkeeper, moved towards the near post, got tangled up with one of his own defenders, and the ball – with a little sigh of apology – plopped over the line. Seven minutes later Ian Pearson scored the goal of the match. Hatch took a long throw, Lee Roberts dummied and let the ball run and Pearson, having first deftly controlled it with a thigh, used his right foot to score with a spectacular overhead shot.

Exeter were now undeniable and three minutes before half-time Peter Rogers touched in the third goal that put the game beyond Newcastle's reach. Ken Wharton, hurt and prostrate on the ground, put, Hatch onside, the Cornflake Kid slid a twenty-yard ground pass in from the left and Rogers was there to stab the ball past poor Carr. 'Que sera, sera', bellowed the crowd . . . 'You'll never walk alone' . . . and then, after some reflection, 'We want four, we want four.' And Martyn Rogers obliged just four minutes from the end, with a left-foot shot that he did not hit cleanly but which still sent the ball crisply just inside the right post.

Four hundred and seventy-five clubs had entered for the 100th FA Cup and Exeter of the Third Division were in the last eight, along with seven members of the First. It was an achievement which John Delve and his team celebrated with lukewarm champagne, while outside the crowd sang 'One team in Devon . . . there's only one team in Devon.' Outside, too, pride lighting up their faces, there were old men who remembered the triumphs of 1931. Now they had a new story to tell.

Meanwhile, Brian Godfrey was giving some thought to the kind of phrase that would look good in the morning papers. He found one in the end. 'We've seen off the Lions, we've beaten the Magpies and now we've got to do the same to the Cockerels', he said. 'D'you get it? Millwall, Newcastle and now Spurs. Not bad, eh?' The papers obliged.

The champagne began to lose its novelty and, as beer took its place, thoughts turned to Tottenham and White Hart Lane. Godfrey was now saying, with Churchillian solemnity, that 'Spurs hold no fears for us.' John Delve, the captain's voice, felt that 'Spurs will be doing the worrying.' Tony Kellow, more than a little grieved that he had failed to score against Newcastle, thought that 'White Hart Lane will be as good a place as any to get one or two.'

Exeter City's allocation of tickets for their engagement at White Hart Lane was 7,500. It was hopelessly inadequate, especially as the club suddenly discovered it had upwards of 30,000 fans who had been passionately devoted to its cause since their long-ago schooldays. Pat Wakeham, City's secretary, even received threatening telephone calls and felt obliged to make his number ex-directory. Brian Godfrey got a letter from a local resident explaining that he had not been able to queue for a ticket because he was in Exeter Prison – just a few hundred yards from the ground. He was being released on the day before the match and, please, would they let him celebrate his freedom by going to White Hart Lane.

Tottenham themselves had grown a few inches since those adolescent days at the beginning of the century when they won the Cup as members of the Southern League. They had become members of the game's aristocracy, a club with a sheen to its name, wealthy, successful, international and still intensely ambitious. They had won the Cup again in 1921, 1961, 1962 and 1967; the League championship in 1951 and 1961 (the first club to complete the League and Cup double in the twentieth century); the League Cup in 1971 and 1973; and, with the coming of European competition, the Cup Winners Cup in 1963 and the UEFA Cup in 1972. They were clearly partial to years that ended in 'one' . . . and here they were again.

Their extravagant side reflected their ambitions. It included Osvaldo Ardiles, one of the men who had helped Argentina win the World Cup three years before, a slight, neat player, quick as a finger-snap in thought and movement, a bouyant, combative, endlessly inventive little chap. They had Glen Hoddle, the most exciting young player in the country, a willowly and elegant Londoner with an element of fantasy in his make-up; Steve Archibald of Scotland, and the black Garth Crooks, one of the best striking partnerships in British football; and Steve Perryman, their experienced captain and chief marshal in defence. They gave Tottenham originality, a style of their own and sharp teeth. They could be generous in defence but the strength of their game was in attack: they lived dangerously and gave a lot of pleasure in the process.

Spurs' expensive tastes were reflected in another way, too. The old, straight-backed main stand at White Hart Lane had been pulled down to make way for a new creation that would look good and make money. All the Exeter fans saw was an open area of mud and puddles, although in the match programme there were pictures and promises about the things to come. The new stand, they read, would include '72 private viewing suites

– commonly referred to as "Boxes" ' which would be leased for three years at £30,000 a time.

Brian Godfrey knew that ambition of this kind was expensive and that Spurs probably needed victory more than Exeter. The North London club wanted an early return on their investments. 'I reckon Spurs couldn't believe their luck when they drew us and we all knew that if they hit their game they could destroy us', he reflects. 'But I knew my lads and we felt that if Tottenham were a bit short on the day we could take them. Their defence wasn't too clever and we honestly believed that what we'd done to Leicester and Newcastle we could do to Tottenham. We knew they wouldn't fancy a replay back at our place. People said we had nothing to lose. That was rubbish. We had a hell of a lot to lose.'

Exeter were at full strength for the tie, with their players on a bonus of £180 a man if they won and the bookmakers assessing their Cup chances at 80-1. Tottenham, the 7-2 favourites, were without the second of their Argentine stars, the large and bearded Ricardo Villa, and also John Lacy in defence. George Mazzon, a twenty-year-old midfield player who had been born in Waltham Cross of Italian parents, kept his place in a side that lined up like this – Daines; Hughton, Roberts, Perryman, Miller; Hoddle, Mazzon, Ardiles; Galvin, Crookes, Archibald.

Rain beat across the rooftops of North London, drifting over White Hart Lane like a heavy mist and laying water on the red track round the pitch until it looked like a moat. And yet, marvellously, it was an occasion of colour and warmth, with the players and supporters of Exeter at the heart of it all. Seven and a half thousand westcountrymen held their own with more than 30,000 Londoners: they filled the Park Lane end of the ground with good humour and indomitable optimism. They were on-stage in one of football's most celebrated theatres and they relished every second of it.

Soon, too, they had reason to hope. Exeter harrassed Spurs in midfield, chasing and covering as if their whole way of life was at stake, and there were even moments when they promised to take the lead. The admirable Delve opened up the Spurs defence for Peter Rogers, only to see Rogers slip and lose a vital split-second, Pearson failed by a forelock to reach a long, slanting centre from Martyn Rogers, and Peter Rogers, once again, drove the ball hard across the face of the unprotected Barry Daines in Tottenham's goal.

White Hart Lane still waited for a goal at half-time and, just sixty seconds into the second half, Exeter had their best chance of the match. Kellow snapped onto a mistake by two Tottenham defenders and found himself with the sort of chance he had been taking with cold certainty all season long. His shot was not a bad one but it still allowed Daines to make a spreading, sprawling save at the base of his right post.

The lights began to dim for Exeter. A wayward boot caught Ian Pearson on the head and, suffering from concussion, he was wheeled out of the game on a stretcher. Reg Pratt took his place and quickly discovered that Spurs were beginning to find their touch and establish their rhythm. Ardiles was full of life, his darting, twisting runs making sharp inroads into the Exeter defence. It was Hoddle, however, who was to prove the essential difference between the sides.

In the 62nd minute Tony Galvin and Ardiles combined for a short corner and the ball whisked to Hoddle whose curving, searching centre to the far post was headed down and into the net by Graham Roberts – his first goal for Spurs. Eleven minutes later Hoddle sent a teasing free-kick into the Exeter six-yard area, Len Bond fumbled it and the ball ran to Paul Miller who scored with gusto and ease. Two members of the Spurs defence – the defence which had been regarded as the soft underbelly of the side – had scored their goals.

It seemed less than justice that an error by Bond should have opened the way for the goal that settled the match. Bond had been magnificent and Martin Dean of the *Express and Echo,* the Exeter evening paper, properly made this point: 'Bond was still suffering the effects of a terrible collision with Archibald when he made his one mistake of the game . . . but typically he refused to make any excuses for his error afterwards. 'I didn't get my body behind the ball and it slipped away from me', he said. It was a travesty that Bond of all people should have been at fault . . . up until then the only thing he had failed to catch cleanly was double pneumonia.' Ken Jones added his tribute to Bond in the *Sunday Mirror:* he named him as Man of the Match.

White Hart Lane rose to Exeter as they left the field, and soon afterwards Tottenham's manager, Keith Burkinshaw, a tall, quietly spoken Yorkshireman, was paying his own tribute to the westcountryman: 'I don't mind admitting Exeter gave me a scare. Full credit to them. They closed us down superbly and stopped us playing in midfield – an area where we normally operate so well. They didn't have any stars but, my word, didn't they work.'

Spurs, of course, went on to win the 100th Cup – the final with Manchester City going to a second game at Wembley, where Ricardo Villa made his mark on history by scoring twice.

So, in the end, the strong arm and the big spear prevailed . . . just as they always have. The Gnome Uniteds and the Outback Albions have fired our winters for a hundred years, but the secret of their appeal lies in the hopelessness of their task.

Jack may have felled Goliath in the first round proper, but what happened to him in the quarter-finals? He probably lost to an own goal and a disputed penalty at Anfield or Highbury.